THE PHYSICAL BODY, THE SPIRITUAL BODY

Physical and Spiritual Bodies Compared

Ainsley Chalmers

BALBOA.
PRESS
A DIVISION OF HAY HOUSE

Balboa Press books may be ordered through booksellers or by contacting:

Balboa Press
A Division of Hay House
1663 Liberty Drive
Bloomington, IN 47403
www.balboapress.com.au
1 (877) 407-4847

Print information available on the last page.

ISBN: 978-1-5043-0496-2 (sc)
ISBN: 978-1-5043-0497-9 (e)

Balboa Press rev. date: 11/17/2016

This book is dedicated to the memory of my wife Denise who led me to Jesus Christ and went to be with the Lord in December 1991.

It is also dedicated to my children Joanne, Nicole, Jacqueline, John (deceased) and my grandchildren Joshua, Matthew, Isaac, George, Charles and my great grandchildren Rubi Rose and Lucas.

I would also like to acknowledge the many who have helped me in my Christian walk and finally to Creation Ministry International (creation.com)who helped by tying up a lot of theological loose ends in my journey with the Lord thereby increasing my faith in God.

A special thanks to my dear friend Dr. Jim Fitzgerald who went to be with the Lord in May 2015. He helped by confirming that the scientific facts presented in this book were solid.

To the ideas and inspiration for this book I give God the glory because without His help it would not have been.

Genesis 1:27. So God created man in His own image; in the image of God He created him; male and female He created them.

Genesis2: 7. And the Lord God formed man from the dust of the ground, and breathed into his nostrils the breadth of life and man became a living being.

Hebrews 11:3. By faith we understand that the worlds were framed by the word of God, so the things that are seen were not made of things which are visible.

Genesis 2: 16,17. And the Lord commanded the man, saying, "Of every tree of the garden you may freely eat; but of the tree of the knowledge of good and evil you shall not eat, for in the day that you eat of it you shall surely die.

1 Cor 15: 44,45,47. It is sown a natural body, it is raised a spiritual body. There is a natural body, and there is a spiritual body. And so it is written, "The first Adam became a living being". The last Adam became a life giving spirit. The first man is of the earth, made of dust; the second man is the Lord from heaven.

Rom 5:12,19. Therefore, just as through one man sin entered the world, and death through sin, and thus death spread to all men because all sinned. For as by one man's disobedience many were made sinners, so also by one Man's obedience many will be made righteous.

James 2:26. For as the body without the spirit is dead, so faith without works is dead.

John 14:6. Jesus said to him, "I am the way, the truth and the life. No one comes to the Father except through me".

Eph 2:8,9. For by grace you have been saved through faith, and that not of yourselves; it is a gift of God, not of works, lest anyone should boast.

John 3:16. For God so loved the world that He gave His only begotten Son, that whoever believes in Him should not perish but have everlasting life.

1 Tim 2:5. For there is only one God and one Mediator who can reconcile God and humanity-the man Christ Jesus.

CONTENTS

INTRODUCTION

I was asked to speak to a Christian group on acquired immunodeficiency syndrome (AIDS) because of my research activity in this area. The plan was that I would give a general address on the scientific aspects of AIDS, such as how human immunodeficiency virus (HIV) kills immune cells in the body, and the epidemiology and spread of the disease. However, while I was writing this talk, it seemed to me that the scientific and medical aspects of AIDS had a spiritual counterpart. This aspect is explored further in chapter 1, "Genes."

The concept that the physical and spiritual may be interrelated was new to me. It probably would be true to say that most people, including scientists, believe the disciplines of science and theology are separate, unrelated, and sometimes antagonistic disciplines. Science is perceived by most to be centred on measurable, physical dimension, while theology is centred on the invisible or spiritual. This perception appears to be flawed, in that the Bible describes historical events like the creation, a worldwide flood in Noah's time (4,500 years ago), the formation of languages and spread of humanity throughout the world at Babel, and a four-thousand-year genealogy of humankind from Adam to Jesus.

The main area where science and the spiritual meet—or, rather, clash—is in the ethical domain, on issues such as in vitro fertilisation, stem cell research, cloning, abortion, euthanasia, and gay marriage.

Beliefs in "young earth" or "old earth" creation and evolution, thought to be unimportant by many in the Christian faith, invariably lead to worldviews that are anti-Bible or atheistic.

In scripture, we find the apostle Paul spoke on the physical/spiritual connection in his letter to the Corinthians: "It is sown a natural body; it is raised a spiritual body. There is a natural body and there is a spiritual body" (1 Cor. 15:44). John 1:13 speaks of a physical birth from human passion and contrasts it with a spiritual birth from God. Also in John, Jesus said, "That which is born of the flesh is flesh, and that which is born of the Spirit is spirit" (3:6).

On many occasions, Jesus used parables to compare the kingdom of God, or the spiritual, with physical events. For example, He compares the kingdom with soil, wheat, tares, a mustard seed, yeast, a treasure, a pearl, and fishing net (Matt. 13:23, 24, 31, 33, 44–47). Jesus also made similar parables to illustrate God's love and forgiveness (Luke 7:44–48, 15:20).

These passages on the interconnectedness between the physical and spiritual expanded the boundaries of my thinking, thereby allowing further scientific/spiritual insights to come. Some of these are expressed in this book. In other words, my experiences in the material, scientific area appeared to have a spiritual component to them.

This revelation was exciting because it opened up a new panorama on the spirituality contained within the physical world, particularly in relation to certain aspects of biochemistry and physiology that were familiar to me.

So the pages of this book initially arose from talks given to Christian people in the Adelaide district many years ago. There always seem to be a few more insights that reveal themselves when one is asked to speak on this subject. As to whether this revelation is from God, only the reader can make that assessment.

My view, as bold as it is, is that the contents of this book are from God, as revealed by the Holy Spirit, because what I have written concurs with God's Word, the Bible. This book is also inconsistent with my usual way of thinking, which is far more scientific than theological. That is, God must have revealed these comparisons between the physical and spiritual for me to even be aware of them.

My hope for this book is that the reader finds this revelation challenging, enlightening, life-giving, and uplifting. But it is the Holy Spirit's job to convince the reader.

Why God may have motivated me to write this book is a big mystery. Most of my writings are research publications. It was never my intention to write a spiritual (or any) book. It cannot be because of my Christian walk, which is far from being as fervent or committed as it should be, I am ashamed to admit. To be honest, I am an old cracked-clay vessel but, nonetheless, still a work in progress for the Lord. On the positive side, Jesus Christ is my Lord and Saviour, and for those accepting Him, salvation is through His sacrificial death on the cross of Calvary over two thousand years ago.

My experience, like that of many other Christians, is that all blessings in this life and the next are through God's grace, love, and mercy, as expressed through His Son, Jesus Christ. Most Christians agree that without God's grace and guidance, we'd have no chance of achieving anything worthwhile anytime, anywhere. As Jesus once said "I am the vine, you are the branches. He who abides in me, and I in him, bears much fruit: for without Me you can do nothing" (John 15:5).

This book is written in a simple, repetitive manner, with as much scientific jargon removed as possible, in the hope of making it easily understood. Despite this, I have attempted to be as accurate as possible without confusing the reader. I have also made an honest attempt to provide a literal presentation of scripture without adding unnecessary meanings.

Allow me to provide a short biographical account, so the reader may assess my academic credentials and understand my background. I was born in Lucknow, India, in 1938, the eldest of five boys. In 1948, we emigrated from India to South Australia, where my parents sent me to primary and secondary Catholic schools.

After secondary school, I worked full-time as a laboratory analyst in the mining industry, while also attending the University of Adelaide. There I earned a bachelor of science degree in chemistry.

After completing my degree in 1962, I married Denise in 1964. We had three beautiful daughters and a son, who unfortunately was stillborn in 1967.

In 1966, a position in the Department of Surgery at the University of Adelaide allowed me to set up a biochemistry research laboratory. This job fulfilled my latent desire to do research in medical biochemistry.

While working full time, I commenced a master of science programme in 1966 at Flinders University of South Australia. The research component of this degree entailed working on the mechanism of action of a clinical immunosuppressive drug called azathioprine. This drug demonstrated clinical success in inhibiting immune rejection of renal transplants. Thanks to expert supervision by my academic supervisors, the late professors Maurice Atkinson and Andy Murray, the research went very well. Because the work exceeded requirements for the Masters program, I was awarded, instead, a doctor of philosophy degree in 1972. This was followed by a postdoctoral fellowship for two years in the cancer area and, later, tenured positions in clinical biochemistry in government-run laboratories.

My research publications have spanned a variety of areas, such as cancer, immunodeficiencies, renal stone biochemistry, anti-inflammatory drugs, AIDS, and the biochemical changes in psychological stress leading to impaired immunity.

My other work-related responsibility was to teach medical students various aspects of medical biochemistry, immunology, and haematology. For this activity, Flinders University of South Australia conferred senior lecturer status upon me.

After about seventy-five research publications and thirty years' experience as a chief medical scientist in charge of a laboratory at Flinders Medical Centre, I retired in 2003. Although retired, there is still some teaching and research in my life, in addition to writing this book.

My Christian training included a Catholic school education as well as four years of experience in various charismatic churches. On July 25, 1977, my Christian walk really took off following a personal touch from Christ after prayer from a Spirit-filled minister. That saw a rededication of my life to Christ, followed by an immediate, life-changing, born-again transformation that only the Holy Spirit can affect in one's life.

Prior to this life-changing experience, my Christian walk was practically non-existent. For me, God, if He existed, was a strict schoolmaster, up there in heaven and just waiting for me to make a mistake. One could never do enough to please Him or experience His reality. In the end, I was a spiritually worn-out person who quit going to church and began to doubt whether God existed. Obviously, His love was not evident to me at that time. First Corinthians described me to a tee: "But the natural man does not receive the things of the Spirit of God, for they are foolishness to him; nor can he know them, because they are spiritually discerned" (2:14).

God, however, was very patient with me. It was the infilling of the Holy Spirit in early August 1977 that made His presence real to me.

In about 1983, I completed a diploma in Christian studies at Vision College in Sydney, Australia, as a part-time external student.

On December 30, 1991, my wife, Denise, died of cancer. I married my second wife, Heather, in June 1996, and by March 2002, we were divorced. The reason for the breakdown was complex; suffice it to say that it is difficult to bring two families with adult and teenage children together.

To the reader, statements such as "revelation by the Holy Spirit" and "knowing Christ in a personal way" may seem super spiritual and heavy. Revelation by God is scriptural (2 Tim. 3:16; Eph. 1:17; Rev. 1:1). It is available to all Christians open to His leading. Revelation does not mean that God spends all His time talking to us. In fact, the only time He spoke to me in thirty years as a Christian was when He spoke the words "Trust me." To me, revelation is when you have a deep conviction to do something, or when something has been a big mystery in your life and then suddenly seems clearer.

Let me give some examples.

One Saturday morning in 1989, while I was lying in bed, the conviction to write this book came out of the blue. There was also the conviction to call this book *The Physical Body: The Spiritual Body.* There were no prophetic words in my ear, just an inner conviction deep within.

There was also a revelation about evolution. This came about through my own background and also by listening to talks by others, both for and against evolution. At one moment in time, evolution just seemed scientifically impossible. Most probably, my newfound Christian walk caused certain doubts and questions to arise. As a new Christian, I initially had a sense that evolution might have been God's plan for creation.

Please do not shut off if you believe in evolution. I fully respect your belief in this area. Salvation does not hang on your belief or unbelief in evolution, but on the fact that Jesus Christ is your Lord and Saviour, who forgives our sins and reconciles us to God (Col. 1:20–22). Nonetheless, some of my scientific colleagues do not believe in God because of their belief that evolution over many millions of years, not God, has created all life forms as we know them today. As such, evolution is a very dangerous belief. It can close your mind to the possibility that God exists.

As you read, please be patient. Try not to let your background, experiences, and biases cause you to shut off what may seem unintelligible or theologically indigestible to you at this moment. Please question and confront what seems hard to digest. I certainly did. The main aim of this book is to share my thoughts on this subject with you and perhaps give you a different point of view. Hopefully, all who read these pages would find this aim met one way or another. It is not my intent to change the basic structures of your beliefs. Only God, working in concert with your logic, can convince you to do that, and only if you need to.

A short introduction is needed to define what I mean by the *spiritual body* and the *physical body.* Most of my concepts in this area have been borrowed from Christian teaching and, to some extent, common sense. Just as this book discusses the physical and spiritual aspects of science, so is a person composed of both a physical and a spiritual body. It is these two beings who make up the human being. The physical being is simply the body with all its very complex systems, such the renal, brain, skeletal, hepatic, cardiovascular, lymphatic, neuromuscular, and many other systems. The physical being, wonderfully created by God though it is, is here only for a short time and then dies because of sin (Rom. 5:12).

The inner being or spirit is invisible and nondissectable. It represents the eternal part of us (John 3:16; Gal. 6:8). In fact the body without the spirit is dead (James 2:26). The spiritual being is the worshipful or intuitive part of us. It is that eternal part made in the image of God our Creator and in essence it is truly who we are (Gen. 1:26). Therefore it represents everything positive and essentially good within us.

The further aspect of our being which is often mentioned in the literature is the soul. *Spirit* and *soul* are probably interchangeable terms. The spirit and the body can be polluted by sinful activities. In scripture there are many examples of people possessed by spiritual demons. This implies a spiritual pollution by satanic powers influencing our minds and our spiritual lives. Similarly, pollutants such as cigarette smoke, alcohol, drugs, and other environmentally contaminating chemicals can pollute the physical side. I believe that drugs like alcohol, ice, LSD, and heroin, which physically affect normal brain function, can also open us up to demonic influences. I discuss this in more detail in the chapters that follow.

This book is not a treatise which knocks the physical part of us as being evil and bad. The physical body is an incredible wonder and, along with the rest of nature, reflects the wonderful, creative, and artistic ability of God. God said of His creation, including us, that it was very good (Gen. 1:31). Unfortunately, because of our sin of disobedience in the garden of Eden and our attempts to do our own thing apart from God, the body became pollutable and eventually died because of sin (Rom. 5:12, 8:10).

In this book, the physical aspect of our being will be described first, followed by an attempt to relate it to the spiritual aspect. As indicated already, Christ is God, who communicates with our inner being through the Holy Spirit and has much to do with its growth and full expression. Hence this book has much to say about Jesus Christ, who to all Christians is God our Creator and the source of our salvation (Eph. 3:9; Col. 1:16; Rev. 4:11).

My prayer is that you receive much positive revelation, blessings, and spiritual growth through reading the pages of this book.

CHAPTER 1

GENES

(a). Scientific aspects

Before launching into this complex section, certain definitions need to be established, because science is a language all its own.

Molecules are chemical substances such as methane (CH_4), one carbon atom combined with four hydrogen atoms. Sugar ($C_6H_{12}O_6$) is another molecule comprising carbon, hydrogen, and oxygen atoms. Common salt (NaCl) is a molecule comprising sodium (Na) and chlorine (Cl) atoms. Polyvinyl chloride plastic or PVC comprises many hundreds of molecules of vinyl chloride (CH_2CH-Cl) joined together chemically. Because it has many repeating units of vinyl chloride, it is called a *polymer.*

Deoxyribonucleic acid or DNA is the genetic material of our cells. It is a polymer located mostly in the nucleus of our cells. It is an information molecule that determines who we are. For example, DNA gives information for brown or blue eyes, shortness or height, our weight, the colour of our hair, the shape of our mouths, the size of our ears, and many hundreds of other characteristics.

DNA is described as a double helix because it looks like two strands of rope wound around each other. This rope strand of DNA is, for functional reasons, divided into smaller pieces called chromosomes.

The information in DNA canbe likened to the information in a book, except the information in the DNA book is made up of only four letters—A, C, G, and T—that follow a specific order. These letters represent four different chemicals whose specific combinations work like a code, the genetic code, to describe us. The information in our DNA book directs our physical characteristics by prompting the body to make different proteins in varying amounts.

There are forty-six volumes compromising the human DNA book. Each volume can be thought of as a chromosome, with the chapters being analogous to genes. Our cells have forty-six chromosomes, twenty-two from Dad and twenty-two from Mum. In addition, we each have an X volume from Mum, and another X volume from Dad (for a female child) or a Y volume (for a male child). Mum's ovum has twenty-two chromosomes plus an X, and Dad's sperm has twenty-two chromosomes plus either an X or a Y.

Our physical characteristics are a mixture of Dad's and Mum's genes, so we usually look like our parents. For example, we may have Dad's nose and ears, Mum's eyes and hair, and so on.

Returning to the book analogy, Dad's chromosome/volume 1 pairs with Mum's equivalent volume 1, his 2 with her 2, and so on. Sometimes, therefore, we are said to have twenty-three chromosome pairs (including the sex-determining X and Y chromosomes). Some animals have more, but most animals have fewer chromosomes than humans.

Cells called *parent cells* divide to create two *daughter cells*. When the cell divides, the forty-six chromosomes have to be duplicated so the parent cell can hand down a complete set to each of the two daughter cells. Nearly all cells in the human body contain these chromosomes intact. (A few exceptions, like the red blood cells and platelets, have no DNA.) The chromosomes are identical in every tissue in our body, be it heart, lung, kidney, or muscle.

So how does this information in our DNA make us who we are? Basically, some chapters in our DNA books code for protein. For example, some chapters, or genes, make more of a given protein, resulting in a profound effect on our eye shape. Other genes do not make proteins, but can control genes that do make proteins.

The DNA information of all human beings is almost the same. The differences between us are probably due to less than 10 per cent of all the information in DNA.

Close relatives who intermarry may have children with deformities. This is because they may both have mutations passed down from a shared ancestor, such as the same grandfather. When two people are unrelated genetically, then a bad gene in one will more often be compensated for by a good gene in the other. Typically, healthy children will result.

The DNA content of a bacterium is shorter than ours. A bacterium has information equivalent to a DNA book 100 pages long, comprising three million ACGT letters. In comparison, the information in human cells is forty-six books containing 100,000 pages, comprising over three billion letters. So for a bacterium to evolve into a human, it must increase its information by a thousandfold, from three million to three billion letters.

It must be emphasised that the ACGT alphabet in DNA cannot give information unless it is ordered, just as the letters A to Z in our alphabet must be ordered into units we call *words* to convey information. To use another analogy, just as your computer is useless unless it has been programmed to do certain tasks, so must the ACGT in DNA must be ordered in a particular sequence to give life. This ordering can be likened to software. Ordering requires intelligence, just as software must be written by an intelligence—a programmer.

(b) Mutations explained

All DNA, in the course of an organism's life, develops errors. As a parent cell copies DNA to make new daughter cells, sometimes spelling errors creep in. There may be the omission of a letter, word, or sentence, or the addition of a letter, word, or sentence. These changes are termed *mutations*, and can change the intended meaning of a gene. For example, the sentence "The cat is black" could be changed to "The cat is back." Mutations might jumble the order of ACGT to give nonsense messages, just as jumbling up the letters in this book would create nonsense words.

Errors can be made when the gene is copied for the daughter cells, or they may happen in the normal lifespan of one cell. In addition, pollutants in our world can corrupt DNA information.

Copying errors in adult cells are called *somatic mutations*. Many times these mutations are present in the germ cells (female egg or male sperm) and therefore are inherited at conception. Such mutations are called *germ cell mutations*. There are over six thousand germ cell mutations reported for humans.

Mutations to DNA information can result in many undesirable effects, such as aging, diseases, and cancer. The reason we age is because our cells mutate.

To counteract damage to DNA information, we have protein enzymes that can repair DNA. They are called *DNA repair enzymes*. The repair system cuts out a mutated letter of DNA and replaces it with a new, undamaged letter identical to the original, undamaged DNA. Over the course of time, however, the repair system cannot keep pace with the repair required, and we accumulate more mutations in our DNA.

The evidence for mutation accumulation over time has been detected in the laboratory. These accumulated mutations result in breakdown of our body systems as we age, until it is so extensive that we die. So mutations eventually result in disease and death.

People with deficient DNA repair systems age very rapidly. Some develop cancer at a young age. Cancers are caused by mutations to DNA in certain key genes. When DNA is damaged, the cell should detect this damage and produce an appropriate protein from the *tumour suppressor gene.* This protein stops the cell from replicating, or forming daughter cells, until the damaged DNA is repaired.

If the tumour suppressor protein is not made, or if the gene that instructs the body to create that protein describes a mutated protein, then no suppression occurs. The damaged cell continues to divide, increasing the number of bad (mutated) cells in the body. This cluster of bad cells may eventually become a tumour.

On our cells, there are *receptors* that are acted upon by outside hormones to increase or decrease cell division. Receptors are also susceptible to mutation. If, as a result of receptor mutation, the cell loses its hormonal brake on growth and continues to divide, the cell will likewise accumulate further DNA damage and can become a tumour.

Certain viruses can insert their genes into ours, causing our genes to mutate and thereby turn our normal cells into malignant cells. Cervical cancer is one example of this. One can now be immunised against this particular group of cancer-causing viruses (called *human papillomavirus*, or HPV) and thereby be protected from cervical cancer.

To summarise, genes give information that determines the structure and therefore the function of proteins, which in turn determine our physical characteristics. Genes can be damaged, resulting in damaged, non-functional proteins or no proteins. This damage is termed *mutation.*

(c). Gene function

The human genome has now been sequenced. Each cell has been shown to contain about 30,000 genes that code for about as many proteins. The incredible thing is that all this information is contained in a single cell, smaller than a full stop. In this day and age of miniaturisation, a cell makes the most sophisticated computer look quite large and cumbersome.

Not all the genes in a cell are actively making protein all the time. For example, if one stops eating glucose for a few weeks, then the gene-derived proteins involved in metabolising glucose will be reduced, simply because they are not needed as much. If one starts eating glucose again, then these proteins will be turned on again.

Similarly, if we reduce our overall sugar intake by fasting, the body adapts by metabolising fat stores more efficiently to meet energy requirements. It does this by making protein enzymes actively involved in fat metabolism.

In some cell types, certain genes or proteins are turned on or *expressed*, whereas in other cells they are permanently turned off, even though the same genes are present in all cells of the body. For example, cells involved in fighting infection (called *lymphocytes*) activate their genes to produce antibody proteins to neutralise infections. In contrast, muscle cells, which are not involved directly in fighting infection, have these antibody-forming genes, but they are permanently turned off. Muscle tissue rarely, if ever, makes antibodies.

Each cell in the body makes only those proteins related to its role in the body. Where a given protein is not required for normal function, that protein is not made. This makes good sense: why make something when or where you do not need it? *Control genes* determine the activity of other genes involved in protein synthesis.

Great tracts of DNA do not appear to have any function, in that they do not code for proteins. These apparently useless genes, once called called "junk DNA," account for over 90 per cent of the information in a cell. These bits have recently been shown to have roles that are very likely to be important to the normal function of the cell.

Some of the junk DNA is believed to be like a dimmer switch on a lamp. The dimmer the lamp, the less protein is made. This junk DNA acts like a control gene.

There are DNA segments called *pseudogenes* that look like normal genes, but do not make proteins. Pseudogenes were thought to be a useless remnant of evolution, genes rendered non-functional by mutations. However, research a few years ago has shown that pseudogenes make products that likewise control the synthesis of certain proteins.

In time, it is very likely that all junk DNA will be shown to have other important roles. Scientists no longer call it junk, as it has demonstrated its importance for normal cell function.

What happens when you have changes or mutations to DNA? If the protein is an enzyme, then its enzymic activity can be unchanged, increased, decreased, or removed altogether. The latter two effects usually occur; that is, the enzymic activity is reduced or deleted.

(d). Chemicals causing mutations.

What are some of the pollutants that can interact with DNA and cause mutations? Among these *mutagenic chemicals* are 3,4-benzopyrene in cigarette smoke and other combustion products, aflatoxins and nitrosamines in food, chromium and nickel as used in the electroplating, and asbestos and radium as used in the mining industries.

Our bodies produce some pollutants, which are called *free radicals.* They are generated from normal metabolism. The two most prominent free radicals are superoxide anion and hydrogen peroxide. Free radicals can also damage our DNA. Antioxidants in our cells neutralise free radicals, thereby reducing damage. Some of these are ascorbate (vitamin C), vitamin E, vitamin A, coenzyme Q10, and glutathione. Free radicals are not altogether bad, however, as many have a role in fighting infections.

It is probably true to say that most mutations are caused by pollution, whether in the environment or in our bodies as free radicals. One of the most devastating effects of mutations is the formation of cancerous cells, and the estimate by reputable cancer agencies is that up to 90 per cent of cancers are caused by pollution. You are no doubt aware that cigarette smoking greatly increases the risk of lung cancer. The Japanese who survived the atomic bombs dropped on their cities in World War II had a much greater incidence of blood-related cancers, such as leukaemia and lymphoma. Similarly, those who survived the Chernobyl nuclear disaster are expected to have an increased tendency to form cancers.

This is a very depressing scenario. But we are all "polluted" in this sense, and thereby mutated in our genes to a greater or lesser extent. In short, we are all mutants.

(e). How mutations cause cancer

There is a better understanding now of how mutations cause cancer, though the fine details are still being researched. It is known that we have in our chromosomes lengths of DNA which are known as *proto-oncogenes.* These genes are under strict control in the cell and are usually expressed when the cell divides. Some proto-oncogenes act as growth factors, regulating the growth of the cell. Other genes called *anti-oncogenes,* or tumour suppressor genes, slow down cell division in order to permit DNA repair to occur. Anti-oncogenes therefore reduce or inhibit the formation of mutations.

If mutations occur in the DNA of proto-oncogenes or anti-oncogenes, the genes produce mutated proteins that inhibit normal controls for cell growth or DNA repair. When this mutation event occurs, the cell as a whole can turn into a cancer cell.

Proto-oncogenes, when mutated, are called *oncogenes,* and it is the oncogene that changes a normal cell into a cancerous one. Mutated anti-oncogenes do not become oncogenes, but their defect means that norml DNA repair is not occurring. This promotes the development of the cancer cell, though it does not cause that development.

In the normal human cell, there are about a dozen proto-oncogenes and anti-oncogenes, most of which, if mutated, can generate cancers.

Viruses can also generate cancer, as we have touched on already. Another well-known virus that acts by a similar mechanism is called HIV-1 or human immunodeficiency virus type 1. This virus is responsible for the disease called acquired immune deficiency syndrome or AIDS. It also has an effect of increasing the incidence of a specific cancer called Kaposi sarcoma.

HIV is attracted mostly to a particular white blood cell type called the T-helper cell, which has a central role in defending the body against invading organisms such as bacteria, viruses, and fungal infections. Once inside the cell, HIV inserts its genes into our genes. It then makes many copies of itself so that it can infect other cells similarly. This process of replication results in the death of the host T-helper cell and spreads of millions of HIV virions to neighbouring T-helper cells. The death of the T-helper cells puts AIDS patients at the mercy of the multitudes of disease-causing microorganisms which are continually waiting to get at all of us, but are normally neutralised by a healthy, functioning immune system.

Spiritual aspects of genes

The Bible has much to say about family trees, especially the one relating to Our Lord Jesus Christ. In Christ's family tree were many famous yet fallible people, such as Adam, Seth, Noah, Abraham, Israel, and David. To my way of thinking, this chapter on genes has two important implications as far as the Bible is concerned, and these are considerations of evolution and salvation.

(a) Initial difficulties

At one time I was a new Christian and staunch evolutionist (termed a *theistic evolutionist*). Comments by some well-meaning Christians that evolution was against what the Bible said about creation made me feel uncomfortable. I tolerated these simplistic comments by saying that these people were not scientists and therefore did not fully understand the evolution story. Also, some Christian ministers agreed with me that the evolution story could be reconciled with Genesis 1. I viewed evolution as God's plan for creating our world and the universe. I bore in mind that evolution is a theory, and that it could possibly be wrong. But until something better came along, I intended to stick by it.

To a scientist, a theory is a way of trying to explain an event or observation. For example, a scientist could have one or many theories about the unusual weather patterns we observe now: that they are due to atmospheric atomic bomb testing, to sun warming, or to global warming. Some of these theories could be partly true. One may be wholly true. All could be wrong. It would be close to impossible to test each of these theories fully enough to be certain.

A theory is different from a fact or a law. A law in science is something which has been proven indisputably by evidence or experimentation. For example, the law of gravity states that we are attracted to the earth by a force equivalent to our mass or weight. We can easily prove the law of gravity by throwing a ball into the air; the law of gravity states the ball will come down because of its mass.

Man-made laws may be changed. For example a right-hand turn at an intersection that was lawful last month may now not be permissible. Abortion was once illegal, whereas now it is legal. This is not the case with natural laws. Natural laws are unchangeable.

Initially, the creation story seemed implausible to me. This in turn caused me discomfort, because the Bible was alleged to be inspired by the Holy Spirit (God), and as such, I believed it must be infallible and contain absolute truth (2 Tim. 3:16). To my mind, the unexplainable parts could be understood collectively as mysteries known only to God, which must be taken on faith by believers. So I put them in the too-hard basket.

Two aspects of the Bible account of creation were difficult for me to reconcile. Firstly, how could the whole of mankind come from one man and one woman when it is a scientific fact that close-relative conception often results in some sort of genetic deformity in the offspring? Secondly, how could man live to be nearly one thousand years old? In the Genesis account, many of the people in the early creation era lived in excess of nine hundred years. This just did not ring true.

The rest of the creation account was digestible. God is God, and if He says that He created the world in six days, then He did. Though God is timeless, I believe that He uses timescales in the Bible that we can understand. That is, His six days are our six days, and not six billion years. Also, in Exodus 20, God commanded humans to work six days and rest on the seventh, the Sabbath (vv. 8–11). It would make no sense to work six thousand days and rest on the seventh thousandth day.

(b). Clarity at last.

Like other creationists, I now believe that God created the earth, the universe, and everything in them in six days some 6,500 years ago. If prehistoric animals came before us and died before the fall in the garden of Eden, this wouldn't line up with God's Word in Holy scripture, which states that death entered this world because of of the sin of Adam and Eve (Rom. 5:12, 8:10). Before the fall, sin and animal death were not in existence. So how could early animals, including prehistoric mankind, die before the fall? Also, when God created the earth and everything in it, he said it was very good (Gen. 1:31). Death and suffering over millions of years are not really "very good" by most definitions.

Noah and the ark was a scientifically plausible event, as was the flood (Gen 6:13-22). Jonah in the belly of the sea monster was also possible (Jonah 1:17). However, relatives intermarrying and absurdly old ages were hard to swallow until God's revelation kicked in. This revelation came from Dr. Carl Wieland, of Creation Ministries International, who was a part of a grand round talk at Flinders Medical Centre in the early 1990s. He opened my eyes and gave me an aha moment.

The explanation of it all goes back to the concept of genes and mutations, which had been staring me in the face for many years. Literally, I had been blinded by the evolution story for most of my life and could not see the wood for the trees.

When Adam and Eve were in the garden of Eden and fellowshipping with God, there was no such thing as mutations, disease, sin, and consequential death in the animal kingdom. Man and woman were completely unpolluted, living in harmony with God. God saw His creation and said that it was very good. Pollution, disease, sin, and death, all not-good events, were set into motion when man and woman disobeyed God and did their own thing. Humans started to change physically and spiritually for the worse from that time on. The whole of creation was affected by death from this sin, and it had other far-reaching consequences.

When humankind was cast off from Eden, their genes were still intact with zero mutations. Brother and sister conception was scientifically feasible due to low mutation rates, without the genetic consequences we have nowadays. When the level of mutations had risen over time to an unacceptable level, God forbade close relatives from intermarrying (Lev. 18:6–17). As mutations accumulated, we see that in the Bible account, the lifespan of humans decreases gradually (compare Gen. 5:3–32 with Gen. 11:10–25). Modern medicine has brought about some prolongation in lifespan since the 1950s but that is only a slight upward kink in the overall trend.

As I mentioned, once mutation frequency increases, lifespan decreases. This has been demonstrated dramatically in patients with an accelerated aging disease called progeria. The revelation helped me understand the longevity and brother-sister intermarriage described in the Genesis account.

Scientific theories about the foundation of the universe have two major flaws, in my view. These flaws are violations of two basic laws of thermodynamics. Note my use of the term *laws*. The first law of thermodynamics states that energy cannot be created or destroyed, but it may be changed from one form to another. Putting it simply, you never get something from nothing.

One cannot make a lump of wood from thin air. A magician may appear to, but you know that that lump of wood was in existence beforehand—he was just hiding it from us. Similarly, that lump of wood cannot disappear as though it never existed. Sure, it can be burnt and converted it into light, heat, and chemical energy, but it cannot just disappear as though it never existed.

This earth and the universe that surrounds us are composed of matter, just like that lump of wood. The first law of thermodynamics says that the universe could not come into existence out of nothing. So where did our universe come from? It sure is a lot of matter.

Scientists can say the universe arose from the Big Bang (if you are a Big Bang theorist). If the Big Bang is a fact, then where did the matter come from for the Big Bang to do its work? The universe, with its billions of galaxies, cannot be sensibly explained by astronomers. Science cannot explain the existence of matter from nothing because such spontaneous generation goes against the first law of thermodynamics. Nothing plus nothing equals nothing.

Matter, therefore, points towards the existence of God as the Originator, the Creator (Gen. 1; Col. 1:16, 17). Only God is able to create something like a small block of wood or this massive universe out of nothing.

The second law of thermodynamics states that matter is in a state of increasing entropy. This means everything is wearing out, breaking down, or running out of useful energy. We all know, for example, that things like cars, lawn mowers, clothes, and ourselves are continually wearing out.

Evolution states that man has evolved from primordial soup in an upward way in contravention of the second law. According to evolution, the atmosphere of this planet was once a mass of gas molecules (where did they come from?) which, under electrical activity in the atmosphere, joined to form more complex molecules. These complex molecules in turn formed the complex biological molecules we know today. These molecules then started to reproduce themselves leading to the formation of the most primitive unicellular organism. This simple organism, under changing environmental conditions involving mutations and natural selection, went on to form more complex organisms. This process continued over many millions of years until eventually the human being developed, the pinnacle of evolution at this point in time.

All this goes against the second law of thermodynamics because it the process goes from higher entropy (gas molecules swirling at random) to greater organisation or smaller entropy (humans).

Also, gases under an electric discharge (or any other input) do not form the chemicals found in living cells. Even if gases could form these chemicals, the chemicals alone could never organise themselves into a simple cell. It is a bit like saying hurricanes blowing through a metal yard for billions of years would ultimately create a Boeing 747 or a computer. The human cell is far more complex than any man-made device—airplanes and computers cannot reproduce themselves.

(c). More detailed biochemistry negates evolution

As a biochemist, I am interested in the molecules that make up life. The molecules in humans are very complex, and each molecule depends on the others for its existence. As already indicated, you cannot have even a minor variation in molecular structure (mutation) without things going bad.

For example, DNA makes another nucleic acid called *ribonucleic acid* or RNA. There are many different forms of RNA, such as ribosomal, messenger, and transfer RNA. Basic messenger RNA consists of up to 30,000 types which code for just as many proteins.

DNA is a huge polymer. It contains a particular sequence of the chemical letters ACGT for each protein it codes for. RNA also is a polymer, derived from these DNA letter-templates. In a fundamental life form like a bacterium, which is by no means simple, the DNA code consists of three million ACGTs. The probability of these bases being strung together in the right sequence three million times to create microbial life is therefore 1 in $4^{3 \text{ million}}$. This is rather small probability—pragmatically speaking, an impossibility. This probability becomes smaller when one factors in all the RNAs and proteins derived from this DNA.

Now consider that in humans, the required number of DNA base sequences are about three billion. The probability of achieving the right ACGTs in the right order through random combinations is immeasurably small.

The proteins derived from DNA and RNA are made up of twenty amino acids, each of which must follow a particular structure; otherwise nothing will work in the cell. Some proteins convert DNA into more DNA for cell replication. Other proteins convert DNA into RNA. Still others use RNA to make more proteins. Some proteins have a role in maintaining the structure of the cell. Some are involved in preventing certain bits of DNA from being converted into RNA. Many proteins are involved in generating energy for the cell. And this is only a partial list of what proteins can do.

As you see, the cell is incredibly complex. Each molecule is dependent on the others. Every one of the tens of thousands of proteins in a cell needs every other protein. All must have precisely the right structure; otherwise nothing will work and the cell will die. The machinery of the cell is so complex and balanced that humans, after spending billions of research dollars, have only a basic understanding on how the cell works.

In short, there is incredible design and balance in the cell. Only God could design anything so beautiful yet complex. To say that it just came into being by chance is the height of improbability. It is, in fact, impossible. It also is a terrible insult to God, our Creator.

Did the protein evolve first, then the DNA, or what? This is an important question because every molecule in the cell is in significant relationship to every other molecule. There is a complex symbiosis in the cell. If you destroy a few molecules, or even change just one, you throw the whole system out of equilibrium.

Evolution requires a scenario in which these molecules were floating about at random. Through the passage of time, whammo, they came together and it all worked and life was born. Suppose that did happen. Where, then, did the cellular membrane that holds the molecules together come from?

Or consider life on a larger scale: human beings. Evolution would have it that early *Homo sapiens* arrived on the scene 100,000 to 200,000 years ago from subhuman, apelike species. According to biblical genealogy, God created us about 6,500 years ago. Death and suffering arriving in the garden of Eden at about this time, resulting from Adam and Eve disobeying God's command. If biblical creation is all pie in the sky, then why did Jesus Christ Himself state, "But from the beginning of creation, God made them male and female" (Mark 10:6)? Jesus also said, "The blood of prophets which was shed from the foundation of the world may be required of this generation. From the blood of Abel to the blood of Zachariah" (Luke 11:50–51). The very words of Jesus show that humankind was present from the beginning of creation, and did not appear millions or billions of years later.

This is very significant because Jesus is God and cannot err. Even as a human, He was truly God and truly man (Phil. 2:6–7). He emptied himself by becoming man, but He was still fully God. Similarly, when I played with my young kids and grandkids, I would sometimes get on all fours, pretending I was a lion, and chase them. But I was still a scientist.

The concepts of a new earth (Rev. 21:1), resurrection (1 Cor. 15:20–22), and justification from sin (Rom. 5:8, 9) all hinge on a proper understanding of the first few chapters of Genesis–that is, on biblical history. If you do not believe the first few chapters of Genesis, then why should the rest of the Bible be believable?

If you want to delve at greater depth into the creation and evolution, visit the link http://www.creation.com.

Biological evolution can be summed up simply: it cannot happen. One cannot go from a microbe with three million DNA base pairs to humans with three billion because, in biology, DNA does not build itself up by adding more and more DNA information. DNA degrades over time, in line with the second law of thermodynamics. That is why we die and get cancers.

The lifespan of humans over the last fifty years has gone up, thanks to medical discoveries like immunisation, drugs like antibiotics, and healthier lifestyles incorporating exercise and balanced diets. But our DNA is degrading. We are estimated to be adding one hundred new mutations in each generation. Geneticists have calculated that the human race probably has one to two thousand years to go to extinction.[1] If the human species had been around for more than half a million years, we should have mutated ourselves out of existence thousands of years ago.

Over time, we are heading on a downward path, genetically speaking. But don't despair. We have the good news for eternal life.

(d). Genes and salvation.

The other aspect of genes which relates to the Word of God is the teaching on salvation. In John's gospel, Jesus talked with Nicodemus, a highly respected priest of the religious sect called the Pharisees. Jesus said that Nicodemus had to be born again in order to enter heaven (John 3:3). Nicodemus appeared to be confused by this term *born again*. It is a term frequently used by Christians. As one might expect, Nicodemus argued with Jesus about how could he get back into his mother's womb and be born again (John 3:4). Physically, it is an impossibility.

---

1 J. C. Sanford, *Genetic Entropy and The Mystery of the Genome* (CITY: FMS Publications, 2008) PAGE.

My understanding about being born again came unexpectedly. In our earthly conception, the genes of our mother and father come together in the sperm and egg and combine to form one cell. This single cell has all the information about the developing child's myriad characteristics such as height, eye colour, and skin texture. All these characteristics are a mixture of the genes of our parents.

Similarly when we are spiritually conceived or born again, the spiritual genes of Jesus Christ and ourselves come together in this second birth. Once this happens, the things of God start to make sense, whereas before they were foolishness. We start to see things through God's eyes. The Bible, once a boring book, comes alive.

At spiritual conception, we develop the spiritual characteristics of God, just as at physical conception, we developed the physical characteristics of our parents. The exciting thing about this event is that it occurs so simply. It is a decision by us to admit our sinfulness to God, repent, reject Satan and all his works, and ask Christ to be our Lord and Saviour and take over the reins of our lives.

Perhaps the classic physical yet spiritual example of this event occurred when Mary conceived of Jesus by the Holy Spirit as she said yes to God (Luke 1:38). In the same sense, we are conceived by the Holy Spirit when we say yes to Jesus. We are transformed by God's spiritual genes, by Christ living within us (Gal. 2:20). Christ's Spirit and our spirits meld into one. Christ in us, and we are in Christ (1 John 4:12–16; Rom. 8:10, 11).

Another analogy came to me one day. The cross with Christ on it is like the sperm, which penetrated the earth (egg) on Calvary's hill nearly two thousand years ago and brought this earth spiritually back to life. Christ's death, like the sperm's demise, allowed us (the ovum) to live on eternally in happiness and joy with our Saviour. Christ's genes and our spiritual genes come together. As a result, we start to express the Christ nature when we become born again. The expression of Christ's genes within us becomes more and more manifest as we feed His genes by hearing and obeying the Word of God. This is just like the natural genes for metabolising sugar, which become turned on as we eat more and more sugar.

Being sensitive to the Holy Spirit of God allows further expression of the Christ life within us, because we get more revelation of the beauty and goodness of who Christ is. If, however, we disobey God and continue in sin after accepting Christ into our lives as Lord and Saviour, this Christ life within us is stifled and cannot grow. The sin genes are further activated (Rom. 6:1, 2; 1 John 3:8–10, 5:18). One could say that Judas was an example of the latter situation. His greed for money and power broke down his fidelity to God, and he betrayed Jesus.

Activation of the sin gene is like turning on the cancer gene or oncogene. Expression of the oncogene is the physical counterpart of spiritual sin. The oncogene results in physical death; sin results in spiritual death, with its eternal consequences.

Christ's genes within us are like anti-oncogenes. They turn off the sin gene—or, better still, prevent its formation—if we allow His power to work through us (cf. Rom. 7:15–17, 8:1, 2; 1 John 3:7–10). No wonder it is said that we must reckon ourselves dead to sin (Rom. 6:2, 11; 1 Pet. 2:24; 2 Cor. 5:17).

On becoming a Christian, one's sin gene doesn't get removed, unfortunately. It tries, as you well know, to reactivate itself, just as the oncogene does, to the day we die. However, with God's help, through the Holy Spirit, we can keep it silent. Without God's help, we have no chance of resisting sin.

This closeness that God requires of us in our relationship with Him is emphasised often in the Bible. For example, many times we are called the children of God which implies a genetic linkage (Rom. 8:16, 17; 1 John 3:2; Matt. 5:9). In one epistle, Paul says it is no longer he who lives, but Christ living within him (Gal. 2:20). Christ said that we are the branches and He is the vine, and He talks of us being grafted in (John 15:5). In order for this to happen, there must be genetic compatibility between our Lord and us. You cannot graft a thorn bush with an apple tree.

The Bible also talks of us having the mark or seal of God (Eph. 1:13, 4:30; 2 Cor. 1:22). This is akin to us looking like our parents. Their mark is on us.

Jesus also spoke of our closeness with Him when He said, "Eat the flesh of the Son of Man and drink His blood " (John 6:53). Christians at communion time re-enact symbolically their oneness with Christ by eating and drinking of Christ's body and blood. Also we the church are called the bride of Christ, once again emphasising our spiritual oneness or union with Him (Rev. 21:2, 9; Eph. 5:23–25).

In all this discussion, it must be stressed that it is Christ alone who has done it all for us. He has given His life for and within us. All that He asks is that we acknowledge our sinfulness, give our lives to Him, and accept Him as our Lord and Saviour (John 3:16). It is a simple decision but one with eternal consequences. God's only motive for doing this is His deep and abiding love for us. He wants us to have an abundant life here on earth and in heaven with Him (John 10:10).

The Bible says that all our righteousness is like dirty rags, and that all have fallen short of the glory of God (Isa. 64:6; Rom. 3:23). In other words, we may be good guys and help those around us; the world may hold us up as examples of goodness. But this will never be enough to get us to heaven, because our goodness or righteousness lags light years behind God's requirements.

It is the precious blood of our Lord Jesus Christ which washes away our sins, reconciles us to God, and gives us the righteousness of Christ (Rom. 5:9; Eph. 1:7, 2:13; Heb. 9:14; Rev. 1:5, 5:9, 7:14). It is His precious blood which gives us meaningful life down here as well as allowing us the reward of eternal life after we die.

Jesus said He has come that we may have life and have it more abundantly. People blame our Lord for all the heartache, sickness, and tragedy in our lives. But it was humankind who turned away from Him in the garden of Eden, and we are still paying the price for this disobedience by coming under the curse of sin. On occasions when the chips are down, it may feel like God doesn't love us. But it is unlikely that God would harm us, because God is love and gave His life for us. Yes, thank God for His patience, forgiveness, mercy, and love, and for the righteousness of Christ imparted to us 100 per cent through what Christ has done (Rom. 3:22, 8:10; 1 Cor. 1:30; Phil. 3:9).

It is not for us to judge others, heaven forbid. God the Creator has blessed us greatly in His creation. Life without Christ loses its excitement. Christ adds that abundance to our lives that He mentions in John 10:10. It comes not in monetary or earthly riches, but in that deep peace of soul which material things can never give (John 14:27; Phil. 4:7; Eph. 2:14).

The fact of the matter is that Jesus is the giver of life to all who come to Him and accept His plan of salvation. It is our deeply personal relationship with our heavenly Father (once again the spiritual/genetic link) which is most important.

Sure, we hear of Christians killing Christians, but those people will someday have to give an account of their murder to Almighty God. As a Christian, one must work at one's own salvation and cultivate those genes of Christ within oneself (Phil. 2:12). What any other Christian does is between them and God. Obviously, if they are wilfully disobeying the word of God, then we, in love and wisdom, need to correct and counsel them, being mindful to pray for them and ourselves as well that we do not stray.

It is God who gives us an eternal life in heaven through His Son, Jesus Christ. When we die, our spirits live on, either eternally in torment or eternally in peace and happiness with our Lord and Saviour Jesus Christ. This joyous eternal life is a free, wonderful, and glorious gift from Almighty God, just as the physical life that we enjoy is a free gift from God through our parents' union. By the grace of God, we have salvation. This Christian life that we are blessed with is a oneness with our heavenly Father. Christ's genes within us have blessed us not only in this short life on earth, but also eternally, in the next life in heaven.

When we look on our children, we can see our characteristics in them. Similarly, when Almighty God looks upon us, He sees His Son, Jesus Christ, in us because of what Jesus did at Calvary two thousand years ago. Just as the Father and Son are one, so also are we one in Christ.

For Christians, this unity with Christ, the Holy Spirit, and God our Father is the essence of the wonder and excitement of being Christian. A deep relationship with our Lord Jesus Christ gives meaning to our lives. It gives us balance in our lives on earth, not to mention the reward of eternal existence and fellowship with God our Father.

And the gift is free. All we have to do is admit and repent of our sinfulness and say yes to Jesus Christ by accepting Him as our Lord and Saviour.

Any life, including the Christian life, is not easy. But with God's help, Christians have a deep inner peace on earth, despite all the hassles. Having lived both lives, unsaved and then saved, Christians know which is the best one by far. God's yoke is much easier to carry than the one the world or Satan puts on us.

All praise and glory to Jesus Christ for His love, grace, and mercy towards us. He is a wonderful God and the source of all that is good in this life.

CHAPTER 2

THE SIGNIFICANCE OF BLOOD

(a). Physical aspects of blood.

Someone once said to me that there appears to be a thread of blood running through the books of the Bible. For example, God was pleased with Abel's blood sacrifice and displeased with Cain's sacrifice of wheat (Gen. 4:3–5). Later we read of God's command to sprinkle animal's blood on the altar of God to expiate the sins of the people (Exod. 24:6–8, 29:16). In the New Testament, we witness the fulfilment of that earlier blood sacrifice for sin when Christ Himself becomes our sacrificial lamb and dies on the cross of Calvary for our sins (Eph. 1:7, 2:13; Col. 1:14, 20; 1 Pet. 1:2). Scripture reminds us that the life is in the blood (Deut. 12:23). In this chapter, the physical and the spiritual significances of blood will be compared.

Blood consists of a pale yellow liquid called *plasma* in which the red and white blood cells are suspended. *White blood cells* are involved in neutralising foreign invaders of the body, such as viruses, bacteria, and cancer. *Red blood cells*, abbreviated RBC, are predominant in blood, being a thousandfold more numerous than white blood cells. RBCs give blood its characteristic dark red colour.

RBCs are derived from a cell in bone marrow called a stem cell. Bone marrow stem cells have the potential to develop into three different functional cell groups in blood. They can become infection-fighting white blood cells (neutrophils, monocytes, and lymphocytes), cells involved in preventing blood loss (platelets), or RBCs. A hormone called *erythropoietin*, produced mainly by the kidneys, directs the stem cells in bone marrow to develop into RBCs. One stem cell gives rise to sixteen fully developed RBCs in five to seven days. Once formed, the RBC is released from the bone marrow into the bloodstream to perform its many functions throughout the body.

To generate RBCs, the stem cell has to undergo four rounds of cell division or replication over a period of about a week. With each replication cycle, the resulting daughter cells become progressively smaller. Eventually the cell loses its nucleus, which is a critical part of the cell because it contains the genetic information that is important to normal cell function (see chapter 1).

RBCs are therefore unique because they lack genes. One would not expect such a cell to live long. However, despite being deprived of its DNA, an RBC will go on to survive for 120 days. It is also the most mobile of all cells, travelling about 2.5 kilometres per day, or 300 kilometres over the course of its lifetime. Not bad for a cell that's one one-hundredth of a millimetre in diameter.

So what does a red blood cell look like? It has a doughnut-like shape, often described as a *biconcave disc*. With this shape, the RBC can fold in on itself, like a hinged tabletop, allowing it to get through gaps that are one-third of its own diameter. This property allows the cell to get into areas that other, less flexible cells cannot.

What does the RBC do? Its main function is to carry oxygen, the life-giving gas, and distribute it to the various tissues of the body. It is obviously true, therefore, that the life is in the blood (Deut. 12:23). Even though every tissue and every cell contributes to the well-being of every other tissue and cell, it is blood which gives life, in the form of oxygen, to every one of these tissues.

The RBCs are not completely autonomous in this function. The heart is needed to pump RBCs around the body, and lungs are needed to refill them with oxygen and remove carbon dioxide from them. Normally, the lungs are inflated with oxygen-containing air. However, when lung function is impaired by injury or disease, such as asthma, emphysema, or lung cancer, then oxygen transfer to the RBCs is impaired. The entire body suffers and becomes tired, basically because of oxygen deprivation.

Within the RBC, oxygen is carried by a red molecule called *haemoglobin*. Haemoglobin consists of an iron-containing molecule called *haem* that in turn is slotted into a larger protein molecule called *globin*. Globin can be likened to a bread roll, with the haem molecule inserted into the roll like a slice of beef. The red molecule of an RBC consists of four haem molecules in four attached globin molecules. Although it is the iron atom in haem that binds strongly to oxygen, the globin helps in this process.

In humans, there are over two hundred mutations reported for haemoglobin. The mutations occur in the globin molecule, resulting in an alteration of its normal bread-roll shape. Some globin mutations result in haemoglobin binding the oxygen too tightly, so it cannot be delivered to the tissues. Other mutations result in oxygen being bound too loosely, so that it is lost before it gets to the tissues. Generally, cells with mutated haemoglobins do not live very long. They are destroyed by other cells in the body. This results in anaemia or low blood haemoglobin concentrations in patients with these mutations.

Oxygen is released by the RBCs and absorbed by outlying tissues of the body, where it does the job of generating the energy molecule of the cell, *adenosine 5-triphosphate* or ATP (discussed further in chapter 3). Oxygen does this by interacting with the products of food metabolism, namely protein, glucose, and fat. This biochemical process, termed *oxidative phosphorylation*, is complex. Without food, you eventually run out of energy (ATP) and die. (In chapter 4, I will discuss the medical consequences of not efficiently absorbing food molecules into the cells.)

To help release oxygen to the tissues, RBCs makes a molecule called *2,3-diphosphoglycerate* or DPG. DPG facilitates the release of oxygen by binding to haemoglobin. Without DPG, the tissues would be deprived of oxygen and work suboptimally because of reduced ATP stores, resulting in reduced energy.

(b). Spiritual aspects of blood.

I think of oxygen as the physical analogue of the Word of God. Jesus once said, "The words that I speak to you are spirit, and they are life" (John 6:63). Peter realised this when he said to Jesus, "You have the words of eternal life" (John 6:68). Oxygen is spiritual in that it cannot be seen. It is life-giving to the physical body by helping to generate ATP, the energy-giving molecule. The Word of God can be seen in written form, but in its spiritual, invisible form, it is eternally life-giving to our spirits. How it does this is a mystery to us. All I know is that reading God's Word, the Holy Scripture, enlivens me spiritually. This is the testimony of many Christians I have met.

The process of RBC formation is symbolic of Christian growth and development. The haemoglobin in RBCs represents the Holy Spirit, the third person of the divine Trinity, within us. The Word of God states that it is the Holy Spirit who teaches and enlivens the Word of God to us (1 Cor. 2:12, 13).

As the stem cell in the bone marrow, on its way to becoming a RBC, loses more and more of its precious genetic material and as it becomes smaller and smaller physically, it gains haemoglobin. Loss of genes and gain of haemoglobin are inversely proportional. In our own walk in life, as we let go of or lose more of what we once considered important, so God is able to fill us more with the Holy Spirit. The more we have of the Holy Spirit in our lives, the more effective will our roles as Christians be. Firstly, we will understand more fully the Word of God, and secondly, we will be able to carry more of the Word of God and distribute it more effectively to others in need, just as the RBCs distribute oxygen.

The essence of the Word is Jesus Christ, the Word made flesh. By understanding more of Him in our lives, we will be empowered to give more of this life-giving Word to others (Col. 1:9–11; Phil. 4:13). Giving the life-giving Word of God may not necessarily mean preaching, although that may be how God will use you. Your attitude of Christ-like love will speak more highly than a thousand sermons. If people want Christ, they may want Him because they can see Him in you. In fact, our lives may be the only glimpse of the gospel that our friends and colleagues ever see.

All Christians are in ministry in one form or another. The molecule DPG represents our attitude or disposition. Are we givers or takers? Do we have God's Word and gifts and hold on to them, or do we distribute them with a loving and willing heart to those in need? It is only by giving that we can be filled up again (Luke 6:38). Similarly, RBCs depleted of oxygen are refilled with this life-giving gas in the lungs.

You do not have to be a pastor or priest or missionary to be in ministry. Once you invite Christ into your lives, then you are empowered by God to become a child of God. In fact we are referred to as a royal priesthood (1 Pet. 2:9).

When God is dealing with us, it can be a very painful process to recognise and give up things and attitudes which have become ingrained and seem precious to us. God, however, replaces our worldly losses and negative attitudes with His presence in our lives. We really gain spiritually through suffering. To the world, we may not seem successful. But what really matters is how God sees us.

One professor colleague called me a Jesus freak when I shared my Christian beliefs with him. I wore that title with pride and honour. It is, by far, preferable to be a Jesus freak than a Satan freak. If you are not fully for Christ, then you are against Him (Rev. 3:16; Luke 11:23).

An RBC becomes progressively smaller as it develops. In the world's eyes, in many respects, we become smaller as we embrace Christ and our aspirations change direction from those of the world. To many in the world, success is gauged by achievements, the size of one's bank balance, and how large one's house is. But those constitute a pitiful scale for measuring success. You are successful because you are made in the image of God. Therefore, you have the potential and goodness of God within you (Gen. 1:26).

As Christians, we hope and pray that the image of God becomes progressively imprinted on us as we walk daily with Him. One day, the Bible says that we will be transformed into the likeness of Jesus as we come before Him (1 John 3:2; Phil. 3:20, 21). You cannot get any more successful than that, can you?

Worldly success is like a wisp of vapour, which lasts for only a very short season. The success of being in Christ has significant eternal ramifications. It also brings a deep and everlasting peace, even down here, which is not circumstance dependant. So if things are tough, hang on. Pray and praise God more. Jesus wants to see your faith and trust in Him grow. Regardless of circumstances, when you are in Christ, you are always successful, because when God looks at you, He sees His Son. Jesus gained victory over the Devil, death, and the world on our behalf about two thousand years ago. So we come from a position of victory, regardless of how we feel or what we may be going through (Rom. 8:35–39; 1 John 5:4, 5).

Worldly success is a noble aim and not an unworthy aspiration. God wants us to succeed in being good businesspeople, artisans, educators, or whatever. When people see your conscientious, Christ-like attitude, this is a great testimony to God. Success will inevitably follow.

However, when we focus solely on success and thereby relegate God to second place or lower, things get out of balance. Our prosperity should be in Christ, not invested in the trinkets of this world no matter how alluring they may be. As the Bible says, "But seek the kingdom of God, and all these things shall be added to you" (Luke 12:31). In other words, give God top priority and centre stage in your life, and everything else will fall into place.

The other interesting aspect of blood is the union of oxygen with iron in the haem molecule. Scripture describes the Word of God as being a double-edged sword (Heb. 4:12). It is like an iron weapon. The Word says this weapon will penetrate deep, to where the joints and marrow meet (Heb. 4:12). The Word of God will go to the innermost parts of our being and cut out the negative attitudes deep within. God would remove these for our well-being, healing, and growth into Him. Growth is a painful process—just think back on your early teens. But from this growth in Christ comes increasing strength, joy, healing, and peace.

Though the Word of God is like a sword, God does not want us to use this sword to attack others. There is not much love in that. Scripture says to remove first the plank or wrongful attitudes from our own lives with the iron of His Word (Luke 6:42).

This is not a request to self-flagellate. We are told to love our neighbour as ourselves (Mark 12:31). Therefore, do not condemn yourself or anyone else. God will convict you or them of any failings, if He needs to. We are commanded to love and not judge, as love is the major key to a successful Christian life. As Christians (RBC equivalents), we need to move ego (DNA) more and more out of our lives. That way, the Holy Spirit (haemoglobin) can move in our lives, and we can become more useful for God in ministering to others.

Another interesting aspect of RBCs is that, after giving oxygen to the tissues, RBCs receive from these tissues an end product of metabolism, a gas called *carbon dioxide.* An increase in carbon dioxide in the body will lead to a condition called *acidosis.* That is, the body becomes acidic. RBCs, with water, convert carbon dioxide to a substance called *bicarbonate*, which helps neutralises acidity. Haemoglobin also binds the acid and neutralises it, thereby allowing cells to function. RBCs release this acid in the lungs by reconverting it to carbon dioxide, which is then blown out into the atmosphere. So

RBCs feed the tissues with oxygen and get rid of acids, which are life-threatening if not dealt with.

As Christians, we need to help release any bitterness (acids) within others and us. With the help of the Holy Spirit (haemoglobin), human bitterness can be neutralised and released. As physical acidity in humans can destroy or inhibit normal, healthy physiological function, so too can bitterness inhibit the full development of our spiritual potential.

Mutated haemoglobins are like Christians who do not have the true spirit of God. Some may hold on to the Word so tightly that they exclude others who need to hear the Word. More importantly, they may withhold love where it is needed. It is important not only to hold on to the Word tightly but also to feed those in need of that Word. We do this through love and support. God promises that He will replenish us as we give (Luke 6:38).

Some may use the Word too freely, throwing it around anywhere and everywhere, mostly to condemn others. For example, when someone is in distress, they may say, "For whatever a man sows, that he will also reap" (Gal. 6:7). Though the passage is scriptural, it should not be used to condemn those already under stress. Job's friends in the Bible were a bit like that in telling him his suffering was due to unrepented sin.

The other mutated spirit is the religious spirit, which says things like "our church is the true one" or "we have more light than other churches" or "unless you speak in tongues, you are not saved." These spirits take the word of God out of context and impose their biases on others, causing those others to come under condemnation.

This is nothing new. Satan attempted to use God's Holy Scripture to trip up Jesus, who is the fleshly representation of the Word of God. Jesus had been fasting forty days and was feeling weak when Satan tried to tempt Him with God's Word taken out of context (Matt. 4:1–11). Jesus rebuked Satan by using the correct and true meaning of scripture. This was in contrast to Adam and Eve, who were conned by Satan using the Word of God cunningly and incorrectly (Gen. 3:1–6).

Jesus was also hassled by the Pharisees and Sadducees, who tried many times to trip Him up by using scripture incorrectly (Mark 2:23–28; Matt. 22:23–32). They had no success, and because of their jealousy and frustration, they had Him crucified.

Jesus got very angry with those self-righteous people. They used the Word against others, but did not themselves live up to the requirements or essence of Holy Scripture. Instead, they put on a pretence of righteousness and holiness (Matt. 23:1–7). As Christians, we need to be on guard to walk the talk, rather than talk the walk like the Pharisees. Actions do speak louder than words.

The other area in which the Word becomes mutated is in the messages that Christians say they get from God. They come out with statements like "The Lord has shown me that you have a spirit of unforgiveness"—or lust or whatever it is they wish to excoriate. These comments, generally untruthful, are ascribed to God and may have a devastating effect on the person targeted.

For example, a person in one church asked me to pray that God would deliver her from a demon that was causing her to be manic-depressive. She was very relieved that her condition was not demon-related. Right there at the altar, I gave her a short course in biochemistry. Afterwards, we prayed for her healing.

In her church some had labelled her as having a demon. They told her that getting rid of the demon would immediately resolve her condition. That's not a nice label to have to carry around: "the woman with the demon."

Another Christian man walked in shame because his wife said that he had a spirit of lust. He went to every reputable deliverance ministry in town for help. They all discerned that he was spiritually OK. He was not a womaniser, but a faithful Christian husband. Nevertheless, for five years he carried this stigma put upon him by his Christian wife.

It is a very dangerous thing to ascribe words to our Lord or to take His Word out of context. Like cells with the mutated haemoglobin, you could have a short lifespan. Using God's name or His Word out of context is taking the name of the Lord God in vain. It is against His commandments. God said that He will not leave anyone unpunished who takes His name in vain (Exod. 20:7). Words from God should edify the church and build up the person.

So if you are judging or pulling down a fellow human in God's name, be very careful. You could be inhibiting the growth of another human soul as well as your own by using God's message unwisely. Use Holy Scripture with much prayer, and be sure that use is directed by the Holy Spirit. We do not want a mutant or satanic spirit to stuff up people's lives.

To conclude, RBCs are a model of what Christians should be to their community. Christians give out life by being a manifestation of Christ. Like RBCs, they are servers, comforting and nurturing those with hurts. They allow sufferers to release those hurts and be healed through an example of Christ-like love.

The other cellular component of blood is the white blood cell. These cells fight infection and foreign invaders of the body, including cancer. They are also formed in the bone marrow, from stem cells similar to those used in RBC production. White blood cells, however, do not lose their genetic material, as do RBCs. They destroy infections by forming antibodies against them or by physically eating them up. Some cells shoot oxygen radicals at the invading organisms. It is all a bit like *Star Wars*.

Likewise, the church sometimes needs to take a fairly aggressive stance against social and moral issues that are undermining our societies, our Christian values, and our family lives. Some of these issues include stands against abortion, apartheid, euthanasia, gambling, pornography, unfair treatment for minority groups, unfair business practices, world and local poverty, and same-sex marriage. We need to take an active stance against unbiblical positions that undermine the values of our society. As a famous man named Edmund Burke once said, evil breeds because good men do nothing.

So let your politician know when you are unhappy about something instead of sitting around and grumbling about it in a self-righteous manner. Too bad if most people in our society disagree with you. At least you are standing up for your convictions and godly values.

Like infection-fighting white blood cells, we can use the Word of God like an oxygen radical. Jesus used the Word often in His preaching to countermand Satan (Luke 4:1–13). He certainly was radical in the eyes of the established religion of His time. In fact, it was this egoistic church that was instrumental in nailing Him to Calvary's cross.

In addition to their aggressive side, white blood cells have a more peaceful function. They release protein factors, which help growth and the healing of wounds. They also release factors essential to the normal development of a fetus and of other white blood cells.

We as Christians need to demnstrate this function of white blood cells. The factors that we must put out for the growth and healing of the community are mercy, love, joy, peace, understanding, and comfort.

Whatever we do in any area of life needs to be done with guidance from the Holy Spirit, which means doing it in a spirit of love. Judging or verbally shooting someone who disagrees with you is not a spirit of love. Having a self-righteous, ego-filled attitude is also far from love.

We can use the Word of God wisely or unwisely. Used wisely, it is life-giving. Used unwisely, it is discouraging and imparts guilt and condemnation.

The best examples of the Word of God should be us, as living examples of that Word. With God's grace and help, each of us is able to slowly develop into a person like His Son, Jesus Christ. That way, we will become members who are more able to reflect Jesus Christ to our community.

CHAPTER 3

GASES OF LIFE AND DEATH

(a). Physical aspects of gasses.

In the animal kingdom, most gases are lethal. There is only one which is essential to life. This life-giving gas is called *oxygen*, and is chemically abbreviated is O-O or O_2. The main role of this gas is to energise the cell by generating a substance called adenosine triphosphate, or ATP. ATP assists hundreds of biochemical reactions in the cell which would otherwise occur less efficiently or not at all, resulting in cell death. Oxygen generates ATP through a complex biochemical process termed *oxidative phosphorylation*. In this process, ATP is produced from the metabolism of foods such as sugars, fats, and proteins.

Carbon monoxide, or CO, poisons the cell by depleting oxygen availability and inhibiting oxidative phosphorylation. These effects reduce the concentration of ATP in the cell. The body requires vast amounts of ATP for its many energy needs, not only in muscle-related activities but also in various metabolic processes. A cell with low levels of ATP or insufficient oxygen will die. That is why oxygen deprivation for only one to two minutes in humans may result in coma or death.

Carbon dioxode CO2, is incompatible with life in animals. It is, however, compatible with life in plants. Plants absorb atmospheric CO_2 and convert it into sugar and oxygen by using solar energy, in a process termed *photosynthesis*. The plant metabolises this CO_2-derived sugar to derive its ATP. We and other animals eat these plants and derive energy from them.

Because CO_2 is not compatible with life in animals, our bodies exhale it from our lungs. After release into the atmosphere, the CO_2 is absorbed by plants This whole process is a cyclical one.

In patients suffering from lung disease, CO_2 is inefficiently exhaled, resulting in increased CO_2 within the body. The trapped CO_2 is converted into an acid called *carbonic acid*, which acidifies the blood and tissues. This increase of acid in the body is serious and may result in death. The human body is intolerant of changes in acidity, technically known as pH or hydrogen ion concentration. For example, the blood normally contains 35 to 45 nanograms of hydrogen ion per litre. A nanogram is one billionth of a gram. With a minor change of acidity to 160 nanograms per litre, the patient will die of excess acidity or acidosis.

Acidosis causes a loss of potassium salt from the cells, so the patient becomes *hyperkalemic*. That is, they have high potassium levels retained in their blood, which can cause death. Additionally, the normal, efficient enzyme functions in our bodies are affected by acidity. Excess acidity ultimately results in impaired enzyme function. Acidosis has numerous, negative side effects on the cells of the body. It is obvious why the body is designed to rid itself of CO_2.

(b) Spiritual aspects of gasses.

The term *bitter* is synonymous with acidity. The bitter taste of lemons is due to their high concentrations of organic acids. Bitterness in a human being describes a person with an acid disposition or hardness of heart. Such bitterness is usually due to unforgiveness.

People hurt by other people or circumstances can be unforgiving and become hard-hearted.

The Bible has much to say, directly and indirectly, about bitterness. In the Lord's Prayer, we are exhorted to forgive those who have trespassed against us, as the Lord has forgiven us (Matt. 6:9–15). In fact the themes of forgiveness and love dominate most of the Bible. It seems one cannot love without forgiving, and one cannot forgive without loving. Forgiveness is therefore a crucial aspect of loving, which in turn is the most essential quality of a Christian life (Luke 7:44–47).

Bitterness in the human heart is caused by an unforgiving, revengeful attitude. It can inhibit the full development of our inner being and spiritual life. It can also sap us of our energy because of emotional pain. If sustained, this emotional damage can cause physical sickness.

When CO_2 gas is released into a confined space, it causes acidity in and can ultimately suffocate humans. Similarly, emotional bitterness can suffocate the lives of those who live near that bitter person. Those who associate with a bitter person can become bitter themselves if they are not emotionally strong or discerning enough to recognise and avoid this negative attitude. Bitterness therefore has an infectious property about it. One must avoid the bitter environment unless one is strong or discerning enough to effect a cure.

Bitter people lose their flavour (vitality) or inner beauty just as physical acidity causes loss of potassium salt from the cell.

In short, one result of bitterness is that a person can fail to reach his or her full potential. Emotional acidity or an unforgiving attitude can inhibit the development of positive qualities in one's inner being.

It is no wonder that the Lord, in His love for us, warns and commands us many times to forgive and love one another (Matt. 18:21, 22). Nonetheless, some justify their unforgiveness by using God's Word against the offending person. One often hears "For whatever a man sows, that he will also reap" (Gal. 6:7) and "He who spares his rod hates his son, but he who loves him disciplines him promptly" (Prov.

13:24). But no matter how one tries to justify a stance of unforgiveness, the Word of God is very clear on this topic—one must forgive and love without any caveats. God knows what is good for us.

God warns us to remove the plank from one's own eye before trying to remove the speck from a colleague's eye (Luke 6:41–42). We are also told that by loving everyone and not judging anyone, we are born of God (1 John 4:7, 8). An act can be judged as unfair or unlawful, but only God has the right to judge attitudes and motives—that is, the heart of a person. If we recognise and repent of our unforgiveness, God will forgive and release us from this burden, and the process of healing can begin. We can begin to blow off this bitterness or acidity like CO_2, and thereby normalise our relationships with others and with God.

Most of us feel compassion not only for those who have been greatly wronged, but also for those who have done wrong to another. It can be very difficult to forgive oneself and live with the heavy weight of guilt. If we are willing, the key to forgiving others and ourselves is found in scripture. This inspiration came to me from a sermon I heard many years ago.

We know the story of Moses, who led the people of God, the Israelites, from bondage in Egypt to liberty in the land promised by God. One day, people complained to Moses that the waters at a place named Marah were bitter and unsuitable for drinking. God told Moses to throw a tree into the water, which then became sweet and suitable to drink (Exod. 15:23–25). Another time, at a place named Rephidim, there was no water. God commanded Moses to touch a rock with his staff, and water suitable for drinking came out of this rock (Exod. 17:3–7).

In the context of these stories, wood or the staff of Moses represents the cross of Christ. If we allow the cross of Christ to touch our hardness, hurts, and bitterness, Jesus makes something useful and sweet out of them, just like plant life converts our physical acidity (CO_2) into sugar and oxygen. The only proviso is that we must be willing to let go of our hurts. We are not asked to forget, which would be very difficult, if not impossible. Time will, however, dim the memory.

Jesus is a wonderful example of forgiveness, not only throughout His life on earth but particularly on the cross of Calvary. He had been physically abused and humiliated by the Roman soldiers. This abuse included a crown of thorns brutally pushed into His head, thirty-nine lashes with a whip, the tearing of His beard, verbal abuse, and spitting and ridicule from the priests and the crowd. The abuse and humiliation came to a peak at the crucifixion (Isa. 50:6, 53:3–5). In addition, and even worse, He took all our sins and diseases on His body (Col. 2:13, 14; 1 Pet. 2:24; Rev. 1:5; Heb. 2:17). He could have sidestepped this excruciating pain of the body and humiliation of the spirit. His heavenly Father would have rescued Him and destroyed all those about Him if Jesus had called on Him.

Christ went through all of this physical and spiritual pain to show God's immense love for us and to deliver us from sin and, ultimately, death (John 3:16). His desire was to reconcile us to God in peace and blessings and love for all eternity (Rom. 5:10; 2 Cor. 5:20, 21; Col. 16:20).

While on earth, Jesus healed the sick, raised the dead, fed those who were physically and spiritituallly hungry, and, most importantly, gave those about Him hope, joy, love, and peace. Jesus was without sin and completely innocent. His death was certainly unjustified, and in fact the most horrendous injustice ever perpetrated (Rom. 5:18, 19). Despite this, as He hung from that bloodstained cross, His body and spirit wracked with indescribable physical and spiritual pain, He cried, "Father forgive them, for they know not what they do" (Luke 23:34). That was the infinite example of forgiveness and agape love.

One can argue that Jesus was God, so it was easy for Him to forgive. Yes, He was God, but He laid aside the Godhead when He came to earth and became fully man (Acts 2:22; 1 Cor. 15:21; Col. 1:16, 2:9). He hurt, He cried, He felt pain, He grieved, and He felt joy. He was an emotional human being like us (Luke 19:41; John 11:35, 15:11). Even before His crucifixion, His emotional agony was such that as He faced the cross,

He sweated drops of blood (Luke 22:44). How many of us have come to that point of suffering and stress in our lives?

Forgiveness is not easy. After becoming a Christian in July 1977, I identified nine people whom I considered my enemies and asked them for their forgiveness. To put it mildly, dialling their phone numbers was very hard to do. But afterwards, I experienced tremendous relief and healing. The peace and love of God absolutely overwhelmed me, to the point of crying.

As a Christian, I have often received unjust treatment. After much soul searching and frustration, I eventually learned to identify the hurt, repent, and then leave any negative feelings and sinful thoughts at the cross of Christ.

Praying for blessings and the salvation of those who have wronged me has helped considerably. Prayer has brought about a changed Christ-like attitude within myself towards them. A loving feeling towards that person may even develop. It is a daily grind sometimes to be a good Christian, but with the Holy Spirit's help, God can effect positive changes to our lives. Almost daily, the egoistic part of me judges people. I have to continually remind myself that God is the judge. God certainly is long-suffering with me.

When a patient can't breathe properly, perhaps due to emphysema or asthma, or has inhaled a poisonous gas such as carbon monoxide (CO), the treatment involves the introduction of pure oxygen to blow off the excess CO_2 and CO stored in the body's tissues. In cases of CO poisoning, the patient must be treated with oxygen delivered at high pressure. This involves use of a *hyperbaric* or high-pressure oxygen chamber. This hyperbaric treatment is necessary; otherwise CO is not completely removed from the body. It seeps too slowly from the internal organs and tissues, causing the patient to relapse later.

In both a spiritual and psychological context, we can be polluted by the CO-like poisons of society, such as pornography, violence, drugs, and child abuse. All these sinful events can have negative effects on our attitudes and can leave us in fear, insecurity, and torment, as well as give us a distorted view of life. If they occur early in life, when we lack the maturity to handle them, they can cause serious psychological damage.

God in His wonderful provision has made a way. He said that He came that we may have life and have it more abundantly (John 10:10). He also said that His words are spirit and life (John 6:63). God's Word is, to the spiritual body, what oxygen is to the physical body. If we allow His Word to permeate our spirits, it will heal us by blowing out the accumulated junk of our worldly lives.

How do you take God's Word in faith? By knowing that Jesus Christ loves you and wants your happiness more than you do. Jesus knows what will make you happy, even though you do not understand what or why He is doing or allowing certain things to happen in your life. His actions are always for your spiritual sanctification and growth into a Christ-like person. Holy Scripture is not a series of dos and don'ts, but a message of love from God. God is basically saying, "Follow my words and you will be happy and blessed." God's laws reflect our sinful nature. Appreciate and be grateful for forgiveness and salvation through faith in Jesus Christ. Understand the depth of love God has for us.

Without being energised, a person cannot be healed. As the physical body requires ATP energy to perform its many functions, so the human soul needs to be energised by God's Word in order to be healed. For the healing process to occur, we need an energised, positive spirit which only the Word of God can give. If we do not internalise God's Word—that is, read the Bible as we would a novel or an interesting story—then it will not do its work fully, though it may still have a positive influence on our lives. God speaks to us through His Word so that we will be changed for the better.

We can experience blocks to receiving God's Word fully. We may have had some satanic involvements or lived lives full of sin. Repentance will remove the blocks to God's Word. Sometimes the block can be low self-esteem, a feeling that we have failed, life has passed us by, we deserve nothing, and God doesn't really love us. That latter comment in particular is a lie from hell. God loved us so much that He died a horrendous and humiliating death for us. To love yourself is in fact one of the foremost commandments of God, along with loving God and your neighbour (Matt. 22:36–40). You are lovable because you are made in the image of God (Gen. 1:26, 27). You are unique and very precious; God will never make another like you.

Feelings of low self-esteem, Satan would have us believe, are a mark of humility. True humility is when you acknowledge God as the source of all your achievements and talents.

Sinfulness and egotism (which includes self-hate as well as self-exaltation) are like the thick mucous that lines the lungs of an asthmatic. They prevent the oxygen of the Word of God from energising you.

Give all the glory to Christ for the unique and wonderful qualities He has built into you. It may help to make a list of your qualities and thank God for them. Like the apostle Paul, we very likely have thorns in our flesh. Like Paul, we must know that God's grace is sufficient for us (2 Cor. 12, 7–9). We must ask God for help with our negatives without magnifying them any more. God wants us to be real and honest with Him.

Knowing that God has created each of us as a unique human being in His image, and that we are all His children, is more than anyone could hope for. It will help transform your view of life and yourself. If you saw your kids running themselves down all the time, it wouldn't make you happy. How much more so for God?

A deep walk with the Holy Spirit will help the Word to penetrate as deep as the bone marrow of our spiritual lives (Heb. 4:12). Faith is the key ingredient in the healing process. Faith, a gift from God, is like eyeglasses which allow us to understand the Word of God more clearly (2 Cor. 5:7; Rom. 10:17; Eph. 2:8). If you have faith the size of a mustard seed, faith that Christ wants the best for your life, then the Word will move the mountains of pollution out of your life and make you whole

(Matt. 17:20). The Holy Spirit indwelling within us allows this faith to grow. He teaches and reveals to us more about the person of who Jesus is (John 14:26; 1 Cor. 2:13; Luke 12:12). After all, He inspired the Bible (2 Tim. 3:16). He certainly knows the correct interpretation. He will make God's Word known to us in a deep and meaningful way—a way that is life transforming, that is depolluting. In a polluted world like ours, isn't it wonderful that we have the greatest purifying and depolluting agent, the mighty Word of God, taught to us by the wonderful Holy Spirit, the third person of the Blessed Trinity? It cannot get better than that.

It is a sad observation that many who have lacked love and acceptance early in their lives become bitter and hurt. Some attempt to numb this pain with drugs. Drugs are usually addictive. Generally too, they are substances chemically opposite to acids, called *bases.* Bases can reduce or neutralise acidity. Heroin, morphine, cocaine, LSD, nicotine, and amphetamines are all bases.

The trouble with these drugs is that they have negative effects on your personality. Sure, they temporarily kill the emotional pain, but at a horrendous cost to your life. The costs of taking these drugs far outweigh the questionable benefits one receives by taking them.

An advertisement I saw at a bus stop a few years ago stuck with me. The ad showed a young man taking drugs. The caption read, "Tim's need for heroin is only exceeded by his need for love." That caption said it all.

Lack of love and acceptance can lead to bitterness and emotional pain. These are partially neutralised by an addictive base. Realising the extent of the love and acceptance Our Lord Jesus Christ has for us is an important milestone in our healing. So great is His love for us that He died a ghastly death on a wooden cross outside of Jerusalem two thousand years ago. Not only that, but He also took all our bitterness, emotional and physical pain, guilt, grief, and sin to that cross. He crucified all those things as well on His body (1 Pet. 2:24; Isa. 53:5).

When we acknowledge our sinfulness and accept Christ as our Lord and Saviour, it is important to tell our loving Father about our fears and pain. He wants us to talk with Him about it, even though He knows everything. He wants us to hand Him all our hurts. As we become aware of His love for us, as we get to know Him more, our pain will diminish. Scripture says that it is by His stripes we were healed physically, psychologically and spiritually (1 Pet. 2:24).

In the healing process, it is important to relate our pain to another human as well as to God. We may need psychological counselling as well. The healing process is gradual, but we have the assurance that Jesus touches our emotional scars immediately. This healing touch continues throughout our lives as we continue to trust in Him and His provision (Mark 11:24, 25). Knowing the extent of His love for us, as expressed in Holy Scripture, and having a personal relationship with Christ through frank and open discussions in prayer will increase our faith and our healing.

Christ's plan is that you may have life and have it more abundantly. So trust in Him. Millions of dedicated Christians can vouch for His wonderful provisions in their lives. The greatest provision is having God in the centre of our lives. It makes all the difference.

The peace Christ gives is deep and lasting. It must be experienced personally. As He said, "Peace I leave with you. My peace I give you: not as the world gives do I give to you" (John 14:27). The peace of the world is transient. Christ's peace starts deep within us. It makes us feel complete. It gives a joy and a deep inner strength, no matter what your circumstances. Christ's healing is real through the love He pours into us.

There are situations pertaining to forgiveness which need some explanation. In situations where a partner is chronically abusive, then for your own physical and emotional well-being, you should leave that situation. By "chronically abusive," I mean that he or she abuses you physically or emotionally and makes your life a living hell, to the point that your self-image is entirely negative and you cannot cope any more. You have to love yourself—and, if you have them, your children—enough to remove yourselves from that toxic situation.

There is little hope for reconciliation if an abusive partner is unwilling to admit their faults and accept change—for example, by going for counselling. It is only when we come to the cross that Christ can deal with our attitudes and shortcomings. We have to be truthful about ourselves and recognise that we need to change.

Though you may leave your spouse, it is very important that you forgive that person and yourself as well. The bitterness and hurt of the marriage must likewise be left at the foot of the cross.

Every domestic situation must be carefully looked at by competent counsellors and assessed accurately in the light of God's Word. Whatever the circumstance, it is essential to love and forgive the erring partner in your heart. Doing so will allow you to rebuild your own life. If possible, explain why it is necessary to live separately. You should of course pray for that partner. Should they come to a full and genuine repentance, then you should accept them back. By their fruits over a period of time, you will know whether there has been a genuine repentance.

The two main players in this drama are you and God. Scripture encourages us to have a close walk with Christ and His Word in order that we may be made whole. At times, a Christian counsellor may be needed to assist the healing process—usually someone you can relate to and feel comfortable with when discussing your problems. A counsellor should be someone who will pray for you and be a support. Such counsellors and friends have been a blessing to me.

On the other hand, some would-be counsellors have lacked wisdom and almost shaken me from my Christian walk. Time will tell whether your counsellor is suitable for you. As with a repentant partner, "By their fruits you will know them" (Matt. 7:20). Be patient, and try not to be judgemental. Your counsellor is as human as you are and needs as much prayer. So pray that God may lead them. A little revelation from God can work wonders and is worth a mountain of human wisdom.

I would like to digress by discussing the symbolism of some of the gases I have discussed. As I said before, oxygen (O_2 or O-O) is like the Word of God because it is life-giving. Its symbol, the O, is a circle without beginning or end, like God. A circular ring is used to indicate our love for someone. The poisonous gases carbon monoxide (CO) and carbon dioxide (CO_2) can be likened to the contaminated Word—a C that is attached to the oxygen. The contaminated Word is scripture taken out of context so that it no longer gives life.

For example, some Christians believe that speaking in tongues is a sign of salvation. They quote a passage from the gospel of Mark to support their belief (Mark 16:17). Some parents won't take their very sick child to a doctor, because they believe scripture tells them that God alone will heal. Some Christians use scripture to prohibit life-saving blood transfusion, since they believe transfusion is a sin and will prohibit entry into heaven.

The other way of contaminating scripture is to quote it but not live by it. It is harder to walk the talk than talk the walk. A man may say that he has forgiven his wife's infidelity, and yet keep reminding her of it daily. Jesus was angry with Pharisees because they quoted scripture self-righteously but never abided by the essence of the law, which is love (Matt. 23:13–36).

It is symbolic that a carbon atom attached to an oxygen atom is black, while oxidising agents containing oxygen tend to bleach or whiten. CO and CO_2, though poisonous, are colourless, indicating that the light overcomes the blackness.

Water has interesting physical and spiritual aspects. It is talked about in God's Word as being synonymous with life. In the physical realm, we can relate to that (John 4:7–15). Water has the formula H_2O or H-O-H. Symbolically, God, represented here by the circle, is attached to humanity, represented by H. Water exclusively quenches our thirst. Likewise, humanity joined to God is life-giving.

The elements of hydrogen and oxygen, when brought together as gases, do not bond spontaneously. If you are foolhardy and apply a spark to this mixture, they will bond instantly by exploding—and form water. It is the energy of this bonding, through hydrogen peroxide or H-O-O-H, that energises spaceships.

God is waiting to bond to us. It just takes a spark from us (a "yes") to do it. Once this bond is formed, like water it is very difficult to disrupt. What will disrupt this bond is chronic disrespect and disobedience to God's laws. A person will demonstrate these only if he or she does not have a deep relationship with God. God will do all He can to deepen our relationship with Him without encroaching on our free will.

Oxygen is called *electronegative.* That means it attracts negatively charged particles called *electrons* from atoms like hydrogen (H_2). When God (O_2) bonds with humanity (H_2) to give life (H_2O, water), He removes an electron from hydrogen (us). In other words, God removes our negativity and makes us positive. Water is balanced—neither acidic nor basic. It is neutral and therefore non-destructive.

There are chemicals similar to water, called *hydrogen sulphide* (H_2S) and *hydrogen selenide* (H_2Se). Sulphur (S) and selenium (Se) come from the same group of elements in the periodic table as oxygen (O). These substances are poisonous gases and have the vilest of stenches (H_2S is described as "rotten egg gas"). In these structures, one could say the element S is symbolic of Satan. There is no substitute for water in cleansing and healing; it is everywhere on earth. Without water, there is no life. Likewise, humanity without our bond to God is also lifeless.

Living the Word of God frees us from pollution in our spirits, just as taking in oxygen overcomes the harmful effects of acidity and poisonous gases. The Holy Spirit helps internalise and bond the Word of God deep in our spirits to energise and set us free spiritually. At the cross of Christ, we repent and lay down our hurts, regardless of who is right or wrong. We need to know that God forgives us and will help give us a forgiving heart towards the other person involved.

Pray God's richest blessings on your enemies. God will release the bitterness from you. He will convert it to a sweet fruit that will feed you and counsel and energise others in similar circumstances.

We decide whether we want to forgive and love someone. It is not for us to avenge; that is God's business (Ps. 94:1; Heb. 10:30). Once we forgive and love others and ourselves, then the peace and love of Almighty God will flood our beings and we shall know true peace. A forgiving and loving heart will deepen one's relationship with God.

CHAPTER 4

NUTRITION

(a) Physical aspects of nutrition.

We have discussed how humans obtain energy through oxygen and food intake. We have looked closely at the significance of oxygen, and now turn our attention to food

Humans need a balanced diet for growth and survival. The major constituents in food are proteins, vitamins, carbohydrates, and fats, all of which contribute to energy and further protein synthesis.

Vitamins are required in a variety of biochemical processes. For example, vitamins B1 and B6 are required for biochemical reactions involving sugar metabolism. Vitamin C, with other reducing agents, protects the cell from damage due to oxidising species such as oxygen and hydroxy radicals. Vitamin C is also involved in the synthesis of a unique amino acid called *hydroxy proline*. This amino acid contributes to the protein/collagen matrix between cells. Vitamin C deficiency leads to a lack of proper extracellular matrix, a medical condition commonly called *scurvy*.

Vitamin A is involved not only in vision, but also in repairing epithelial cell damage and ensuring normal cell development. Vitamin A deficiency leads to impaired vision at night (night blindness). Vitamin D helps in the absorption of calcium for bone synthesis. Vitamin D deficiency results in rickets, a condition in which the bones become brittle and break easily. Vitamin K is used to activate certain proteins involved in blood coagulation. Vitamin K deficiency can result in excessive blood loss and death.

Vitamins B12 and folate are used for the synthesis of red and white blood cells and other rapidly dividing cells in the body (mouth and gut). A deficiency of these vitamins can result in anaemia and other serious medical complications.

For normal body function, a balance of all nutrients is needed. Despite what some may say, such as that sugar and cholesterol are bad for you, we do need some of these "bad" constituents in order to maintain normal body health. It is only when our intake of these foods exceeds our requirements that they can harm us. Conversely, a deficiency in a food group will lead eventually to clinical problems. Deficiency may not necessarily be caused by poor dietary intake, but by abnormal metabolism of that intake.

Most people are aware that the hormone *insulin* is produced by the pancreas and enables energy-producing *glucose*, a sugar, to enter certain cells. Lack of insulin results in the person being unable to absorb glucose. This condition is called *diabetes mellitus*. One variant of this disease is called *mature-onset diabetes* because the symptoms generally manifest in adults. The patient produces insulin, but his or her cells are resistant to its action. Another variant is called *juvenile-onset diabetes*, because the symptoms usually manifest in children. These patients have lost the ability to produce insulin because the pancreas has been damaged by antibodies produced by the patients' own bodies. This variant of diabetes is therefore considered an *autoimmune disease*.

A major effect of diabetes is the accumulation of glucose outside of the cell. This excess reacts with proteins to form *glucose-protein adducts*, or, as they are sometimes called, *glycated proteins*. Glycation of proteins can contribute to a variety of detrimental clinical conditions, such as vascular, heart, eye, and kidney diseases.

Because diabetic patients cannot absorb glucose into their cells, glucose concentration rises in blood. The body tries to get rid of the excess by excreting it in urine. Hence people with diabetes urinate more than healthy people do. This is why diabetics frequently become thirsty as their blood glucose levels rise.

Poor metabolism of protein is another condition that can result in serious medical problems. Proteins are composed of smaller molecules called *amino acids*, which, if not properly metabolised, can create many medical problems. For example, if the amino acid cysteine is not absorbed normally by the kidneys, it may precipitate in urine, creating cysteine stones that can cause kidney damage.

Malabsorption of fats from the gut can also result in serious medical consequences. In normal diets, calcium binds a small molecule called *oxalate* in the gut, thereby inhibiting its efficient absorption into the blood and eventual excretion in urine. With fat malabsorption, excess intestinal fat binds more calcium. As a result, more oxalate is therefore absorbed from the gut and excreted in urine. In the urine, this excess oxalate will precipitate as an insoluble calcium oxalate salt, resulting in the formation of kidney stones. Malabsorption of fats may also result in deficiencies of the fat-soluble vitamins A, D, E, and K.

A protein called *intrinsic factor* is made by stomach cells and is used to bind and help absorb vitamin B12 from the gut. A key function of vitamin B12 is the production of red blood cells. Patients who lack intrinsic factor and consequently normal B12 absorption eventually become B12 deficient and anaemic, a condition called *pernicious anaemia*. Their blood haemoglobin levels become low, and they become very tired due to low oxygen perfusion. The treatment is an intramuscular injection of vitamin B12, replenishing the patient's low B12 stores and bypassing the deficient intrinsic factor pathway.

Previous research I have done with colleagues showed that patients unable to absorb vitamin C efficiently tend to form kidney stones over and over again. Unabsorbed vitamin C is converted to oxalate in the gut. As previously described, this oxalate eventually precipitates from the urine to form oxalate kidney stones.

Many clinical conditions are characterised by either poor metabolism or poor absorption of certain foods. This in turn results in serious medical complications, which can cause considerable pain and discomfort, and sometimes death.

(b) Spiritual aspects of nutrition

In the Bible, Jesus refers to two foods from heaven. One, called *manna*, fed the Israelites in the desert when they left Egypt with Moses (Exod. 16:35). The other is a food which is spiritually good for us. Jesus says that He is that spiritual food. He states that anyone eating His body and blood will not die, but have eternal life (John 6:53, 54).

At this stage, many of His followers left Him, probably because they thought He was advocating cannibalism. What Jesus was implying was that He is the Word of God sent from heaven. Anyone taking this Word into the depths of their spirit will be spiritually energised for eternity.

Jesus stated that His words are spirit and life (John 6:63). The Bible also says that the Word of God will get down into the innermost parts of us if we allow it (Heb. 4:12). To emphasize this further, Holy Scripture says that the Word will even pierce the division of soul and spirit.

This Word has a wonderful effect on us. Jesus says rivers of living water shall flow out of our innermost being (John 4:10; 7:38). Water is a necessity of life. The living water that Jesus was talking about is the Holy Spirit (John 7:39). With the Holy Spirit or living water in our lives, we can help heal and cleanse those around us. The Word of God is, without doubt, the most wonderful and only real food for our spirits. It takes the Holy Spirit to make God's Word real to us.

It took me more than forty years to come to that realisation. The Word of God was always in our home in the form of a huge, gold, Catholic Bible. We dusted this Bible and, now and then, dared to open its hallowed pages. In those days, five minutes' reading was enough to send us to sleep. The book was unreal, a fairy story. How could the whole population come from one man and one woman? Ridiculous. (See chapter 1.) It seemed inconceivable that the whole world could flood or that a man could live in the belly of a whale for three days. How could Noah get all those animals into one boat without them eating each other? What about evolution? Did it not discredit the whole Bible story of creation?

In my so-called wisdom, I formed the conclusionthat the Bible had some interesting stories but did not bear any relevance to this modern day and age. However, the words of Jesus had a nice ring to them. He seemed a good bloke, doing a lot of miracles and good things which helped those about Him. But that was two thousand years ago.

At the same time, I wasn't sure what really was relevant for today. Perhaps science and technology were? Yes, Jesus was a good bloke, but He was God and not really one of us struggling mortals. Sure, the Jews had been a bit stupid, putting Him on a cross. Perhaps they were jealous of Him or perhaps they were just plain thick. Anyway, who cared? There were so many other interesting things to do in life, like go to parties and get drunk. Or kick a football or play golf.

There was no harm in these activities—except perhaps getting drunk. But these superficial thoughts summarised my view of the Bible.

It was also true that my life seemed to be leading nowhere. There was an emptiness there, which I tried to fill up with things that did not satisfy or give a lasting peace: materialism, alcohol, and infidelity. These things fed the flesh and not the spirit. I was an intellectually orientated person who thought I had figured out the logical way to go. On the surface, I looked happy and successful. I had a lovely wife, three gorgeous daughters, a good job, and a nice house and car. This facade led to a great deal of frustration and pain, not only for me but also for those close to me. Inside, I was a tormented person. Outwardly, I wore a mask of happiness and success.

A major change occurred in the thirty-ninth year of my life, on July 25, 1977, when I gave my life to Christ and accepted Him into my heart to be my Lord and Saviour. It was one thing to call Christ "Lord" in church once a week. It was another thing to mean it in the depths of my being. With this decision made, a deep peace immediately came upon me, one I had previously never known.

A few days later, on August 3, 1977, my Christian walk received another boost when I received through prayer a fresh infilling of the Holy Spirit, of the kind described in scripture (Acts 1:5, 8, 2:38, 4:31; Luke 3:16). With these two experiences came the close presence of the Lord in my life. I knew without a shadow of doubt that Jesus is the way, the truth, and the life, and that any other options life held were not worth consideration.

The Word of God became real to me. All my misconceptions disappeared. These were exciting times, fed and brought to life by His Word. My spirit was enlivened and energised. This gift was from God. He promises it to those who ask in His name. There was very little effort on my part. I simply made the decision to admit my sinfulness and invite Him into my life in a deeper way, with the prayer help of a pastor. His grace did the rest. I knew at that moment that I was now His child, that His seal was on me, that my salvation was eternal and a sure thing (Eph. 1:13; 2 Cor. 1:22; 2 Tim. 2:19). Cleanliness and purity became part of my being, not because of myself, but because of Him. I was voracious for the Word of God, hungry to learn more.

What has all this got to do with nutrition? In my pre- or early Christian life, I felt a need to work to gain merit or favour with God. Over the years, this wore me out spiritually. It became a chore and a frustration. I could never by nature meet the requirements of the law. God, to my way of thinking, was a hard taskmaster. I was like the apostle Paul, trying to do good but being frustrated by falling down all the time (Rom. 7:8–10).

As with malabsorption of nutrients, if we do not take the Word of God fully into our beings, then we can develop spiritual stones.

These stones can cause a great deal of pain, just like kidney stones do. Spiritual stones impede the flow of living water from Christ, preventing us from clearing out the pollution. Like diabetics, we lose water and become dry and thirsty spiritually.

When you allow the goodness of God to permeate your innermost being, you really feel nourished. All you have to do is to receive God's blessing. If you do not allow the fullness of God to permeate you, then you are not absorbing His spiritual nutrition fully. It is there, but you lack the receptors to take it into your being—or rather, you are unaware of your receptors. You just have to be willing to receive from God. He does the rest. It is a gift. It is His grace, earned for you at Calvary two thousand years ago and ever-present today.

As Christ promises, out of you shall flow rivers of living water. These waters clean out the rubbish in your life. They heal and nourish you. If these waters are not flowing, then you develop spiritual kidney stones. The junk in your spiritual life cannot be cleared. You feel contaminated. A great deal of spiritual pain and morbidity is expressed in your emotions.

Yes, we need to absorb fully the Word of God and live it. It is the one instance where gluttony is allowed. We cannot have enough of the Christ life expressed in His Word. The Word truly is spirit and life to us.

Absorbing the Word of God is also like absorbing iron from our food. You'll recall that iron is an important part of haemoglobin, which is in our red blood cells. I compared haemoglobin to the Holy Spirit. As haemoglobin carries oxygen to our tissues, so does the Holy Spirit carry the Word to our spirits.

There are many food constituents which inhibit the absorption of much-needed iron from the gut. One group of culprits are acids such as phytate, tannate, and oxalate. Without proper absorption of iron, we cannot make red blood cells. We become anaemic, and as a result feel weak and lack energy. The best-absorbed form of iron is the haemoglobin present in meat and fish.

Iron represents the Word of God and haemoglobin the Holy Ghost. To absorb the Word of God into our spirits, we need the Holy Spirit attached to the Word. All other things (intellect, worldly pollutions, bitterness, pride) in this world tend to inhibit this process.

Also, acids in food inhibit iron absorption. In our spiritual lives, the acids of unforgiveness and bitterness, unless resolved, will inhibit the full absorption of the Word of God.

Before I came to Christ, there were people in my life whom I considered "my enemies." I felt hey had done me wrong, and in no way was any forgiveness due to them. After I came to Christ, the Holy Spirit prompted me to ring up each one and ask them to forgive me for my negative attitude. This wasn't an easy process. However, having done it, the peace of God flooded me and there was a huge spiritual release within me. My tears of joy and peace flowed, releasing me.

A number of things may block this nourishment from God. Maybe our intellect is so highly tuned that we have rationalised God almost out of existence. God is not revealed to the intellect. He communicates with the inner being or spirit. Our intellect interprets the revelation of God to the inner being and must be subservient to it.

There is nothing wrong with development of the intellect. It is a good, worthwhile pursuit. Most importantly, it is a gift from God which He encourages us to use (Prov. 1:2, 7, 4:5, 9:9, 10:14, 17:27). But it must be balanced, not allowed to rule the whole person.

A colleague of mine is a brilliant scientist. With great excitement, I shared with him my recent Christian conversion. He impressed me by quoting great slabs of scripture and related how he had spent twelve years of his life in a Christian school. My initial rejoicing turned to confusion when he told me he was an atheist. For a long time this news was hard for me to figure out, until I realised that the Word of God was in his head but not his spirit or heart. Since then I have met three other people who attended Christian schools throughout their childhoods and now are atheists.

I discussed this sad state of affairs with a Christian friend. He pointed out that these people had been immunised against a Christian walk because of their "Christian" schooling. I pondered this strange comment. Immunisation uses a dead bacteria, similar to the live one but not infectious, to induce an immune response and thereby confer immunity against that particular bacteria. Likewise in certain schools, maybe the Bible is presented in a dead way. It may not be taken literally or may be presented as a fairy story. Or it may be presented in a way that implies that science has shown that parts of the Bible are not true.

In my experience, one needs to realise that the Bible is absolute truth and as such is a truth above any other. Only when I came to that realisation was I able to allow the Word of God to fully permeate my being.

Science is fallible and changes over time. Holy Scripture, inspired by the Holy Spirit, never changes. It will even outlast heaven and earth (Matt. 24:35).

The theory of evolution sounds very plausible and palatable. It is popular with most academics and intellectuals. I have found it a major trap that prevents people from coming to Christ. It certainly was for me and many of my scientific colleagues. As you go into the truth of it, you will find it is the greatest lie perpetrated by Satan.

If the Word of God describes something—such as creation—I warn you not to throw it out. God's Word is the truth, and anything which contradicts it is a lie. It has taken me many years to find this out. Just remember that "the foolishness of God is wiser than men; and the weakness of God is stronger than men" (1 Cor. 1:25). In God is "hidden all treasures of wisdom and knowledge" (Col. 2:3).

Another intellectual trap is to point the finger at ministers or Christians who have fallen and use their example to justify why one wouldn't want to be a hypocrite like that. In other words, we throw out the baby with the bath water. Our walk with the Lord should be steadfast regardless of who falls. God is not going to judge us on whether some minister fell from grace. He is going to judge us on whether we have truly repented and accepted Him as Lord and Saviour. If someone falls, we should pray for and support them. They are human and must be hurting. God said that we are not to judge others, as that is His realm (Deut. 32:35; Ps. 94:1, 2; Heb. 10:30).

Another block to accepting Christ is sensibility. Individual experience creates damage that can bias understanding. Catholic nuns and brothers were my schoolteachers. In those days—the 1940s and 1950s—religious were often cruel and beat us incessantly for minor misdemeanours. One brother used to make me stand on my desk and shout to the whole class that I was a donkey while he whacked me repeatedly on the legs with a cane. Later, I learned that scripture shows a donkey was a Christ-bearer on Psalm Sunday. So being a donkey was not so bad. Other teachers humiliated me before the class by nicknaming me "Rajah" and asking if an elephant brought me to school, since my family had recently emigrated from India. It was a bit much for a ten-year-old to cop all this nonsense.

If human males have abused us, we may be distrustful of God because He is portrayed as a male figure in scripture. We can come to healing by having a full understanding of the unconditional love of God. Most importantly, we need to forgive those who have hurt us in the past and ask God to bless them. My healing came through counselling, repentance, prayer, and laying on of hands.

Perhaps we have grown up with only a little love in our lives. We have never been mothered and cuddled. The lack of these experiences can make us feel unworthy and cause us to shut ourselves away from the love of God, the love of others, and the love of ourselves. People with hurt sensibilities sometimes try to kill the hurt with suicide, alcohol, or drugs. A close friend of mine tried all of these. Thank God he survived and is now going on with Christ as a whole person.

Perhaps we have suffered for years from asthma, and our lives have been debilitated by it. Maybe we have lost loved ones through accident, divorce, or sickness, and are bitter for this reason. Perhaps we see the misery and suffering of humanity and wonder about the so-called love of God. Often people blame God in these situations and harden their hearts towards Him.

Suffering is a part of our fallen state. It entered the human race after Adam and Eve disobeyed God. But suffering does play a positive role in making us more compassionate. We must accept it when it comes, as it ultimately helps us in our growth and learning about life and God. Suffering helps us understand more fully what Christ endured on our behalf at Calvary. As the Bible says, "All things work together for good to those who love God, to those who are called according His purpose" (Rom. 8:28). Hiding will not make suffering go away. We need to face it and be wholly aware of it.

Christ suffered as a human being for us and out of love for us. He can therefore empathise with us in our suffering. Perhaps, more importantly, I can empathise with Christ and others through my suffering. The whole gospel story shouts life and not death. Christ is a life-giving person (John 10:10). He uplifted all who came to Him. His words are spirit and they are life (John 6:63).

Finally, God's ways are not our ways. Sometimes it gets very frustrating and counterproductive to try to figure out why things happen. Just let God be God of your life. God is love, and we can fully trust Him (1 John 4:8). Accepting the mysteries is part of the faith walk with Christ. God made this very clear to Job in chapters 40 to 42. If we are bitter against God, we have to repent and ask His forgiveness. Also, we have to forgive ourselves.

Is my life bliss since becoming a Christian in the true sense of the word? Unfortunately, no. My marriage of nearly twenty-eight years ended when my wife died of cancer at the young age of forty-eight. She died while I was trying to start writing this book. My heart was shattered by it for many years. I loved her dearly. She was instrumental in my becoming a Christian, and was a continual inspiration of faith. I praise God for the gift of her life to our family.

Through my intense grief, a lot of emotions surfaced. The Lord has had to deal with a lot of my childhood hurts and a lot of programmed wrong thinking in my intellect. Repentance and forgiveness have become a daily ritual for me. Praise God that I am growing more and more into Him through all of this pain from the past.

As the Lord has said, "He who has begun a good work in you will complete it until the day of Jesus Christ" (Phil. 1:6). Nearly all of us have had a lot of emotional pain to cope with. We are buoyed by the knowledge that the God of this universe is love, and He is with us always. He lives in us and He loves us more than we can ever begin to realise. He is continually healing us day by day (1 Pet. 2:24). That is His plan and that is His nature. His Word abides and helps us grow in our inner being. He nourishes us day by day. And so we praise Him continually for His mighty grace and mercy and peace.

CHAPTER 5

THE SIGNIFICANCE OF SALT

(a). Physical aspects of salt.

There are many salts in the human body. They are found all over, in blood, organs, tissues, and limbs. Outside the cell, the most prominent is a substance called *sodium chloride*, or common salt. Within the cell, another salt called *potassium chloride* has the highest concentration. Other salts include ammonium, magnesium, and calcium salts.

The salt I shall refer to the most in this chapter is sodium chloride. This is the salt we have on our dining tables at home and use as a flavouring agent. Salt can be crystallised from water to give a beautiful cube-shaped crystal. Salt crystals transmit light, even low energy or infrared light. It reflects light from its crystal faces, and this is what gives it its diamond-like beauty. Salt crystals are used in the laboratory because they have the unique property of letting through light from a large proportion of the energy spectrum. By comparison, glass will only allow a narrow window of visible light energy to pass through.

Salt has antiseptic properties when dissolved in water. Some of us have gargled with salt when we had a sore throat, or used salt to get rid of mouth ulcers. The curative properties of the sea are attributed to its salt content. Salt can be used as a cleaning agent. Perhaps its greatest use is in the kitchen, where it is used as a flavouring agent. Salt is also used for preserving certain foodstuffs or for pickling.

In human blood and other tissues, salt plays a very important physiological role. It is present in blood plasma at a concentration of about 8.4 grams per litre. This is nearly one level teaspoonful of salt for every litre of blood plasma. Salt's function in blood and cells in general is to maintain *osmolality.* What this means is that if salt concentration gets too low or high, then blood cells will die by either bursting open or shrivelling up. Even before this point is reached, the patient can become very sick and die with only a minor change of about 10 per cent in blood salt concentration. Salts are also involved in transmitting signals from the brain through the nerve cells to the receptor tissues such as muscle.

When you get thirsty, it is because the salt concentration in your blood has risen. The thirst centres in the brain recognise this change and urge you to drink water. Conversely, when you have drunk too much water and your salt concentration is too low, your kidneys get rid of the excess water.

Salt in all its functions is associated with water. You taste its flavour because it dissolves in the water on your tongue. If salt were as soluble as sand, it would not have any flavour. In its physiological role, salt is dissolved in the water compartment of blood and cells. Wherever salt goes, so does water, and vice versa. So if the body loses salt, it also loses water. If it loses water, it also tends to lose salt.

(b). Spiritual aspects of salt

The Bible refers to salt when it talks of us being the salt of the earth (Matt. 5:13). What does this mean to me as a scientist? Many things.

First, it means that we, as Christians, transmit and reflect the beauty and light of Christ. Like normal salt in the physical world, we allow the full light of Christ to shine through our spiritual lives. How do we do this? "We" don't. It is something God does in us if we are willing to be used by God.

Like salt, we may have to be reformed or recrystallised to fully reflect the beauty of Christ in us. Being boiled in a solvent and recrystallised can be a painful process. However, the Bible says that God disciplines those whom He loves (Prov. 3:12; Rev. 3:19; Heb. 12:6). The Word of God also states that God is the Potter and we are the clay (Jer. 18:6; Rom. 9:21). This implies that God is continually working on us. This theme of God working on us is taken up in Philippians, where it says that God will complete the good work that He has begun in our lives (Phil. 1:6). God never quits working on us in love, because of His compassionate nature.

Second, like normal salt, Christians have a cleansing, preserving, and healing effect on our neighbours and society in general. We do this through praying, being sociable, being there for people in need, listening, and comforting others. My belief is that if God took all the saints off this earth, anarchy would rule. That may happen when those devoted to Christ are raptured off the earth in the end times (1 Thess. 4:16, 17; 1 Cor. 15:51, 52).

Christians truly devoted to God have a positive effect on their society. That sounds a bit self-righteous, but imagine the world without Mother Theresa and her helper nuns, or the Salvation Army, or the St Vincent de Paul Society, or many other such charitable groups. I am sure that there are Christians apart from these groups who have a ministry that only God knows of. It may be that they are helping only a single other human being. But that is what God has called them to, and they are faithful to that calling. There are people who work unnoticed in the church. For example, those working in the crèche tend to the young and change their dirty nappies. These are the unsung heroes. Great will be their reward in heaven. To be the salt of the earth is to be like Christ: obedient to the Word of God, and doing good and godly deeds to those in need.

Before Jesus began His ministry, He was empowered by the Holy Spirit when He was baptised in the Jordan by John the Baptist (Luke 4:1). The Bible says that the Holy Spirit descended on Him like a dove (Matt. 3:16). The Holy Spirit can be symbolised by water. Christ said that out of us shall flow rivers of living water (John 4; 10. 7:38, 39). The living water is the Holy Spirit in our lives. In our physical bodies, salt and water always go together. When we are doing what Christ wants (being the salt of the earth), then the Holy Spirit (water) will be there to guide us.

As a new Christian of about six months, I was asked to speak to a young person who had been on drugs and was contemplating suicide. Normally, my mind would have been blank. However, on that day, in a conversation with him, the words flowed effortlessly from my lips. I spoke about what God was saying about his problem. That night we went to a church service, and the pastor in his sermon repeated almost word for word what I had told the lad that afternoon. The lad came to Christ at that service and is still being used by the Lord more than twenty years down the track. He got rid of his loaded rifle the following week. To God be the glory for his conversion from death to life.

If we operate without the Holy Spirit's guidance, then we become like a high salt concentration. We are all good intentions, but not led by the Lord or sensitive to His leading. It is difficult to imagine the opposite—that is, being full of the Holy Spirit but do nothing when presented with a situation in which help is needed. The Holy Spirit always prompts us to do good works, or to be the salt.

The Bible says, "Faith by itself, if does not have works, is dead" (James 2:17). Our faith works through God's guidance. How do you know that God is guiding you? The words we speak, if in line with the Word of God, are encouraging and loving. They flow easily from our lips. We know that the wisdom is godly because we know we don't have that level of wisdom under normal circumstances. That has been my experience in a number of situations. In other words, I have basically learned spiritual truths while helping someone else.

In the Bible, the second place where salt is mentioned is in relation to Lot's wife (Gen. 19:26). Lot was Abraham's cousin and lived near the twin cities of Sodom and Gomorrah. These towns were very evil places, where God's laws were openly flouted by all. God had had enough of their sin and decided to destroy them.

The only righteous people in the cities were Lot and his family. God sent angels to warn Lot to get his family out of that place before God destroyed it. The angels told them not to look back as they left. Behind them, God destroyed Sodom and Gomorrah. Lot's wife looked back and was turned to a pillar of salt.

Lot's wife, by disobedience, lost the presence of water or the Holy Spirit, and dried out. Similarly, we will dry out in our Christian walk if we keep looking back and continually bemoaning the past. We will become ineffective as Christians unless we are obedient to God's leading and continually filled with the living waters of God's Holy Spirit and His Word.

We, with God's help, are able to reflect the healing, beauty, and flavour of God in our lives and in our society. Only God can do that in us if we are willing. We need the water of the Holy Spirit and his leading in a balanced way if we are to be effective in the ministry of Christ.

CHAPTER 6

THE BODY AS A WHOLE

(a). Physical aspects of body function.

Various tissues in the body cooperate to allow normal functioning of the whole. Breakdown in any one tissue, even to the extent of an impaired single enzyme reaction out of many thousands of good ones, will result in ill health.

Take a situation in which you are placed in imminent danger. Let's say a car driven by a drunk is coming at you fast. The body responds in a number of concerted ways. Your eye or ear perceives the danger and relates that to your brain. The brain rapidly interprets the danger and activates the muscles for running by using the nervous system. The pituitary gland sends out a hormone called ACTH, which is picked by the adrenal gland, which immediately releases a hormone called cortisol. In addition, the brain stimulates the adrenals to release another hormone called adrenaline. Both hormones then go to the muscle, liver, and fat stores to stimulate the breakdown of fat and sugars into energy (ATP). Your lungs cooperate by breathing in more oxygen, and your heart beats faster to get the oxygen around the body quicker. The energy expended and the metabolic activity associated with this expenditure generates considerable lactic acid. To prevent elevated blood acid from occurring, the liver converts the lactic acid back to glucose for further energy needs.

So you see in the process of getting to safety, many tissues cooperate in the body. This cooperation is geared towards one aim: supplying the energy required to run.

The body is able also to heal itself when subjected to a traumatic insult, again through collaborative effort by several tissues or organs. Let us assume that the surgeon's scalpel has to make a number of cuts in the process of removing diseased tissue. The cut tissues then have to be stitched to prevent bleeding. Despite the skill and care used by the surgeon in this operation, it really is the body which is intimately involved in the healing process.

After surgery, the cells near the incision release substances which close or narrow the blood vessels at the site in order to stem the blood flow. *Platelets*—small cells in the blood—are attracted to the site of bleeding, where they clump together. More than twenty blood proteins cooperate to form a fibrin plug around the platelets, further inhibiting the bleeding process. Platelets clumping together are like an iron mesh, and the fibrin plug is like cement poured into this metal lattice.

Most of the proteins involved in making the fibrin plug are made in the liver. Vitamin K is involved in activating several of these proteins. If the body lacks just one of these plugging proteins or is deficient in vitamin K or platelets, then the clotting process will not function. The patient will bleed to death unless these missing proteins are replaced through transfusion.

Along with this elaborate plugging process, the cells of the immune system converge on the damaged site to fight off any foreign invaders, such as bacteria, viruses, or fungi. After the bleeding has been stemmed, the body uses a different batch of proteins to dissolve the fibrin plug and promote tissue regeneration. Once the damage has been repaired, the proteins used in healing degrade, and everything returns to normal. The process of clot removal is called *fibrinolysis*, the opposite of the coagulation involved in the formation of a clot.

So the healing process, like the flight response, involves a host of different cells.

Tissues not only cooperate with one another but also communicate with each other. The flight example showed how the muscle cells are mobilised by electrical and chemical impulses released from the brain, and how the pituitary gland communicates with the adrenal gland by releasing chemical hormone messages.

The *pituitary gland*, which is only the size of a pea, is located directly under the brain. It is the main tissue for sending hormone messages to many other tissues and organs. The pituitary in turn is controlled by another part of the brain called the *hypothalamus*. The hypothalamus releases factors which causes the pituitary to release some of its hormones. One factor interacts with a tissue to release another factor, which may in turn affect another tissue. Cell-to-cell communication is going on in the body all the time, the cells chemically talking to each other.

The pituitary is the main hormone-producing tissue in the body, although other tissues also produce hormones. One of these is the *pancreas*, which produces insulin and glucagon, hormones involved in glucose metabolism. An inability to produce insulin results in the cell being unable to take in and metabolise glucose, which we call diabetes.

Research has shown that cells located next to one another communicate through physical contact. Molecules flow backwards and forwards from one cell to another through specialised *gap junctions*, which exist in the outer cell membrane at the point of cell-cell contact. When this cell-to-cell communication is broken down, as it is by substances called *tumour promoters*, then these cells have the potential to become cancerous.

When one cell fails to do its job properly, this can affect other cells in the body. To use an earlier example, when the gut cells fail to absorb and metabolise vitamin C efficiently, this can lead to the formation of kidney stones. Thus a malfunction in the gut cells can affect the kidney cells.

In addition to the brain sending out chemical signals to other tissues, many of these tissues communicate back to the brain to let it know whether they require more or less hormones. This process is appropriately known as the *feedback loop.*

It should be stressed that no organ in the body is autonomous. They all rely on one another, no matter how important they may be, and this includes the brain. Red blood cells and the hepatic and cardiovascular systems are required to feed the brain oxygen, glucose, and purines so that it can perform its many functions.

The cells of the immune system illustrate cell-to-cell cooperation beautifully. When a foreign microbe enters the body, cells called *macrophages* digest it. The macrophages present the digested portion of the microbe to cells called *T-lymphocytes*, which cooperate with cells called *B-lymphocytes* in helping to make a specific antibody against that microbe. Going forward, this antibody coats the microbe whenever it appears again in the body, which makes it more appetising to macrophage cells. Should this microbe invade even years later, the body's lymphocytes will remember and eradicate it even more rapidly.

This is the principle by which immunisation works. In immunisation, dead bacteria are introduced into the body, usually by injection. Because the bacteria are dead, they can cause no harm to the patient. Nonetheless, the body will form antibodies against these bacteria as though they were alive. If dangerous live bacteria attempt to invade this patient later, they will be rejected rapidly because the immune system has been primed to fight them.

There are many cell types involved in fighting infection in the blood. These cells include T-helper, T-suppressor, B-lymphocyte, macrophage, dendrite, neutrophil, natural killer, and cytotoxic T-lymphocyte cells. These cells, produced by the bone marrow, are fine-tuned in the bone marrow and thymus for their job. The liver supplies nutrients for their growth, and the spleen, thymus, and lymph nodes store them while they mature.

White blood cells produce chemicals called *cytokines* or lymphokines which allow them to communicate with each other. Suppressor lymphocytes help quieten down the immune system after it has done its job. In autoimmune diseases, lymphocytes attack and destroy the body's own healthy tissues, thereby causing disease. Suppressor cells can act as a balance so that the immune system does not get out of control.

This is just one example of an overall scheme of immunity in which different cells communicate for a common good of restoring health to the body. Everything works in a concerted, balanced fashion for the good of the body. In AIDS, the T-helper cells are destroyed by HIV, so the entire immune system crumbles and the patient dies of multiple infections. Antibiotics can give some help to kill bacteria, but without the immune cells working together, infection wins and the patient dies.

Some of the drugs used in transplantation inhibit cell division. Others inhibit the release of cytokines or chemicals used in cell-to-cell communication. As a result, the immune system is depressed or suppressed, allowing the transplanted organ to survive. These drugs are called *immunosuppressive agents.*

This process of communication also occurs within or inside the cell itself. For example, the nucleus makes a molecule called RNA which is transported by other proteins to the cytoplasm of the cell. In the cytoplasm, RNA is met by complex proteins called *ribosomes* in an area of the cell called the *rough endoplasmic reticulum.* These ribosomes, by interacting with the RNA, make a protein whose structure is determined by the information contained in the RNA. This protein is either used by the cell or is assembled into packages for export out of the cell. The packaging is done in areas of the cells called *Golgi bodies.* The packaged protein is transported along the endoplasmic reticulum for export.

Thus, in the normal functioning of the cell, there is cooperation among many subcellular structures. Without this cooperation, the cell would not function and would eventually die. The net result of cellular non-cooperation would be a very sick person.

(b) Spiritual aspects of whole body function.

In the Bible, we hear of the church being the body of Christ (Eph. 5:30; 1 Cor. 12:27). Christ is the head and we are the members making up this body (Col. 1:18; Eph. 5:23). Each member, we are told, has a specific task. Metaphorically speaking, some members compose the eye to see, some the ear to hear, some the nose to smell, and so on. Each member has a specific function to perform for that church to work well.

As the head, in the physical sense, has a major role to play in motivating the rest of the body, so Christ is the spiritual head of the church. It is Christ who should direct where His church will move, when it will move, and how it will move—the activities it will get involved in. As frail, imperfect humans, we need to follow God's directions for all activities.

Different people within the church are involved in different functions, yet they are all under the headship of Christ. The headship of the church on earth should be sensitive and obedient to the leading of the Lord. It is always a bit risky when only one person hears from the Lord for the rest of the church. Messages from Christ should be felt in the spirits of the corporate leadership. One must expect some dissension because of the nature of the human intellect, but there needs to be a spiritual discernment by the majority of the group. Reliance on God through prayer allows God to communicate what He wants for His church. And God's communication comes through the spirit or inner being of a person, not the intellect. This is not to put down the intellect. It has an important role to discern and interpret what is coming from the Holy Spirit.

There are many functions within the church. Among them are to help financially those who are less fortunate, to neutralise erroneous theologies, to counsel people with issues to resolve, to assist with ethical questions, to evangelise, to look after babies in the church crèche, to help with children's worship, to guide the youth, to clean the church, and to be involved in the church music. We may not have one specific task. One can clean the church and also evangelise.

Similarly, cells in the body may also have a multifunctional role, such as the red blood cells or the liver. One must be careful not to emphasise the importance of one task over that of another. Sight, for example, is very important to our normal function, but so also are our hearing and the proper functioning of our gut tissue. One cannot place one above another. They all have important roles to play and contribute to the overall vitality and functioning of the body. This is all common sense, but it needs to be said.

Another important aspect of the church is balance. In the Bible, Revelation chapters 2 and 3 talk about churches with right theology but not much love, whereas others are full of love but their theology is light. The body needs balance as well. It must have the right proportion of nutrients; otherwise it will not function efficiently. The body excretes the useless end products of metabolism in order to function properly. Similarly, the church needs to ignore junk theology and the empty criticism of others. It needs to concentrate on what is positive and nutritious for its continued growth, such as the Word of God. The church must be an extension of Jesus to the world, so that through us, people in and outside the church may be set free.

A weakness we Christians sometimes have is a tendency to gossip about others whom we feel are not quite up to scratch. If you disagree with a person, take it to them in love. Take it also to the Lord in prayer. A group full of gossip and innuendo is like a patient with an autoimmune disease in which the cells of his body attack one another. It leads to a seriously diseased state which could result in death. Likewise, the spiritual body will suffer unless the gossip is controlled.

Nonetheless, the church needs to critically evaluate where it is going. The members need, with God's help, to continually assess their attitudes and repent of the negative ones if they want to be effective like Christ in their lives and ministries. By being more Christ-like, we will be more effective in helping and loving one another along life's difficult paths. We need to build each other up, not by criticism but by encouragement.

In my experience, one sometimes meet well-intentioned Christians who get words from the Lord which "allow" them to criticise others. Those critical words are definitely not from the Lord. In fact, they are breaking the third commandment of God—that one should not take the name of the Lord our God in vain (Deut. 5:11; Exod. 20:7). It is a very serious business to say "God showed me" or "God told me" unless you are absolutely sure it's true.

Sometimes it seems that God is talking to everyone but you, and that can be upsetting. The only words God has spoken to me since 1977, when I gave my heart to Him, were "Trust me." God more often communicates an impression, such as my motivation to write this book. His words give life and encourage us, as they do in scripture. If a person's word is not encouraging or uplifting, then that word is probably not from God. And they certainly are not from God if they contradict His Word in the Bible. So it is very important to discern what the head (Christ) is truly saying to the body (His church). Wrong messages can upset the body just like a pituitary tumour can.

If there is a Christian person who is blatantly living in sin, then we, the body of Christ, must tell that person, in truth and love, that sin is toxic to spiritual health. If that person continues in sin, that is his or her choice. We must always show love and not talk of sinfulness. With prayer and an example of love from us, that person may return to God's plan, which will certainly not happen if he or she is criticised or assessed by us in a self-righteous way.

We are responsible mainly for removing the plank from our own eye. We are not responsible for other people's attitudes. If anyone breaks God's laws, then there will be a consequence, as surely as breaking any human law results in a penalty. The only antidote for breaking God's law is to repent and ask God for His forgiveness. If we don't, then God's laws will break us eventually, as I have found out the hard way.

We are always thankful to God for the well-balanced Christians who accepted us in love and helped us through our sorrowful times. Who were friends when needed. Who were real. Thanks too go to God for the Christians who almost screwed up my life and walk with Christ. It underlined how fallible we all are. Like the cells in our bodies, we need to be sensitive to each other and be Holy Spirit wise in giving right messages to those who need them.

I'd like to relate a personal story which epitomises what this book and what Christianity are all about. When I was going through my valley of despair and grief after my wife died, it just seemed that there was no one able to help heal my pain. I came to the conclusion that this was part of my cross in life.

About two months after my wife's death, there was a notice in the church mail, advertising a grief course. Folks running the course said my condition was too raw for me to do it. My initial thought was "What a bunch of heartless creatures."

Eight months later, they rang and accepted me for the course. I was a bit uncertain as to whether to do this programme, as some of my grief had subsided—or so it seemed to me. Eventually I did enrol in this course, called Beginning Experience. My sad thought at the time was that my weekend was probably ruined.

That weekend in October 1992 turned out to be one of the most precious weekends of my life. All the people on this course had experienced grief from the loss of a spouse, including the counsellors. They opened up their feelings of despair, loss, rejection, and anger. In short, they shared their pain openly with one another. Sensitive communication, hugging, and healing resulted. There was so much crying and healing from long-stored emotional pain. People ministered to one another in their shared grief. So many of my own tears flowed that I had to take Monday off as a sick day due to a headache. My eyes were red and swollen. And I am not the sort of person who cries easily.

That weekend was the turning point of my grief. It allowed me to shut the door on my life and marriage with Denise, and to start my life anew. (I must be honest and admit that the door is opened every so often for a little peek back). It was a gradual healing, and it took weeks, but that weekend was the starting point. God knew my need and got me there with the right people, despite my doubts.

About ten months after that course, I met a lovely person named Heather. We married on June 15, 1996, about four and a half years after my wife's death. Unfortunately this relationship dissolved four years later due to unresolvable clashes among family members. This devastated me and compounded my earlier grief.

Where does God come into all this process? First of all, He made us. He built healing into our bodies and spirits, because God is in the business of healing. Just read the gospels—or better, the whole Bible—if you have any doubts. You will find that Christ's total ministry was one of love and healing.

Christ uses the love of others to help us heal one another. There is much that has been sung and written about love. My experience is that it is a powerful healing force. I guess this is to be expected, since God is love and all those who fully love are in Christ (1 John 4:16–17). By "fully," I mean loving God, our neighbour, and ourselves.

God, when He made us in His image, said that we, along with the rest of creation, were very good (Gen. 1:31). Since Adam and Eve first disobeyed God, we have lost a lot of the "good" that God first described in us. Christ's precious blood redeemed us, and our relationship with God was re-established. God has commanded that we must love God, our neighbour, and ourselves. Then and only then will we truly live. If we pull ourselves down all the time, then we are like an autoimmune disease in which the white blood cells destroy their own body's tissue. Yes, our righteousness is like dirty rags. But if we are in Christ, then we have the covering of His righteousness and are made worthy (Rom. 8:10, 5:18, 19, 4:3, 24, 25). There is "no condemnation to those who are in Christ Jesus" (Rom. 8:1).

I have avoided discussions on the demonic or satanic world in this book, mainly because my emphasis is on the love of God for us through His Word and the ministry of His church. Unfortunately, there is a satanic world out there. Jesus many times in the Bible had to deal with it (Mark 9:25; Luke 8:28, 29; 1 Pet. 5:8–9; 1 John 3:8; Eph. 6:12). In fact, one of the main aims of Jesus's ministry, described time and time again in the gospels, was to set people free from the negative demonic influences with which we are bombarded with on earth.

Satan will try and get into people's lives and then will try to destroy those people, in stark contrast to Jesus, who gives life in abundance (John 10:10). In the Bible, Satan is described from the very beginning of time as a liar and a murderer (John 8:44). Satan has a structured army of helpers who are the fallen angels, or demons, who rebelled with him in heaven (Matt. 25:41; 2 Pet. 2:4; Luke 10:17–19; Eph. 6:12). Jesus basically annihilated the negative forces of Satan and his army by His death and resurrection (Col. 2:15). We have that Christ-derived power if we believe on the Lord Jesus Christ and have faith in what He has gained for us (Matt. 10:1; Mark 3:14, 15, 6:7, 16:17; Luke 10:18–20).

The only power Satan has is the power we allow him to have. Satan is a master of deception. He gets into people's lives in subtle ways, such as through Ouija boards, tarot cards, séances, dabbling in astrology, fortune telling, and so on. Before my salvation, games on Ouija boards were part of my recreation. In hindsight, it was after the Ouija games that my spiritual life started to decline. It was a slow but a very definite decline over about ten years. When I later came to Christ, prayer and repentance for playing this so called "harmless" board game were required for my spiritual detoxification.

Gaining release from any demonic involvement is very simple: repent and ask God's forgiveness. If you haven't accepted Jesus to be Lord and Saviour of your life, then this is the first step for deliverance from satanic influences. You can ask the Lord, after repenting, to forgive you and release the influence of Satan in your life. At the same time, ask for a full infilling of the Holy Spirit to complete your spiritual healing.

You may need the help of a Spirit-filled Christian or several church members to help you in this prayer. Repentance from satanic activity is usually a very quiet pray. Hollywood would have us believe that there is much screaming and frothing at the mouth, as shown in the movie *The Exorcist.* Sometimes when someone has become involved in demonic activity in a deep way, there may be a bit of a battle. By and large, it is a quiet process. After prayer, you come away with the overwhelming peace of God. There is no more torment in our lives, thanks be to God our Saviour. When you pray and believe in the name of Christ, then Christ will set you free. Fill yourself daily with the Holy Spirit. Satanic forces will try and gain re-entry if your spirit is empty of God's presence and the influence of His Word (Matt. 12:43–45).

To recap, Satan has a body of believers, just as there is a body of Christian believers. Satan's army kills, steals, and destroys people's lives whereas God's army gives life in its full abundance (John 10:10). When you are in Christ, Satan should not have any influence in your life. Oh yes, the Devil will try and fool you or get friends and other family members to pull you down. Just remember that we fight not against flesh and blood, but against principalities and powers of darkness (Eph. 6:12). So go away and bask in the love of Almighty God and focus on Jesus. Do not waste your life or time pondering Satan.

This spiritual fight that we have with the demonic is similar to attacks that the body has when bacteria and viruses try to enter our tissues. God through immunity has given the body the ability to fight and destroy these microbes. Even though these microbes are invisible to human eyes, they are visible to our lymphocytes, who recognise and destroy them. When our bodies are run down and in need of rest, then these microbes can make us sick. In this situation, we go to bed and take antibiotics. Eventually our bodies recoup and destroy the infection, and we feel well again.

Similarly, Satan and his demons will try and pull us down and destroy us by guilt, low self-esteem, or other subtle and devious schemes. Satan generally uses people close to us to try and stuff up our walk with God, especially if we are being used in an effective way by God. God however, through the Holy Spirit, has given us the spiritual eyes to discern this invisible demonic activity and to destroy it, using the Word of God and deliverance prayer.

St Paul, a spirit-filled Christian, stated he was aware of Satan's devices and advised Christians how to resist him (Eph. 6:10–12; 2 Thess. 3:3). Sometimes when we are spiritually weak or sick, Satan may gain a temporary upper hand. In this instance, we need to turn to Christ in prayer, repent, receive God's forgiveness, and meditate on the Word of God. Prayer and the Word of God can neutralise these negative spiritual influences.

When we are attacked in an area that we have been attacked in before, we are more attuned and immediately reject this additional attack. This is somewhat akin to immunisation, in that the body will remove the second attack of a microbe much faster because it is primed to do so.

As Christians, we need to communicate with and praise God often in prayer. A friend of mine once aptly suggested that prayer is our two-way channel with God. Prayer with God is similar to the body communicating with the brain. We, the body of Christ, need to communicate with our head, Jesus Christ. We need to praise Him for His wonderful goodness, as He is the fount of all that is good. This praise is akin to the physical brain receiving sugar and oxygen from the body cells. Christ is more than worthy of our appreciation, praise, and thanksgiving. We think of God as being self-sufficient. But He wants a deep relationship with us because He loves us. By praising God and even quoting the Word of God to Him in joy, we allow full passage for God to minister back to us. This praise of God results in a normal, balanced, and healthy functioning of the body of Christ.

In prayer, we can tell God of our needs. He knows them, but He wants to hear from us, just like the physical head needs communication from the cells about the hormone status of the physical body. God can heal you through your prayer contact with Him. Prayer is a powerful force in our lives.

We have the wonderful example of Jesus, who often slipped away to a quiet place to communicate with God (Mark 1:35, 6:46; Luke 5:16). In fact, it is recorded that Jesus prayed all night to His heavenly Father (Luke 6:12). We also have the example of many great saints of God who were persistent prayers, people like Mother Theresa, Martin Luther, William Booth, and Charles and John Wesley. A strong prayer life is the mark of a God-fearing, God-trusting Christian.

To have a close relationship with God, we need to talk to Him often. It is similar to us communicating with our loved ones. Our relationship with them and our understanding of them grows through communication.

When my walk with God has been a bit weak from time to time, it has mainly been because my prayer life has been eroded, whether by laziness or by the woes and worries of the moment. It is amazing, but when you get into sustained prayer and praise to God, your worries do not seem as large. Try to give God half an hour in prayer daily. It truly will revolutionise your life dramatically. Having a penitent heart is important to an effective prayer life.

Jesus thought prayer was important. He encouraged and taught us how to pray, and gave us many examples of His commitment to prayer (Matt. 6:9–13; Mark 11:24, 14:38). If prayer is important to God, then it surely is important to us. Prayer keeps the channel open. Without it, communication becomes blurred. The saying "seven days without prayer makes one weak" is so true.

At the end of this book, it seems appropriate to summarise some of the basic tenets in God's Word which will result in balance and healing to your life. These basic tenets are epitomised in the words *balanced love.*

- Just as in the body, which places the head first and then other tissues in a certain order under the head, it is important to have your priorities in the right place. Put God at your head, then yourself, your family, your job, and your ministry. For example, if you are asked to preach in a church and it clashes with your daughter's birthday party, then decline the preaching engagement. If you are offered a job which means a substantial promotion but involves unchristian activities, then put God first and decline the job. It is very important to have your priorities in the right place; otherwise you will find your life becoming unbalanced.
- Love the Lord your God, your neighbour, and yourself. The scripture for this also applies to priorities mentioned above (Mark 12:30, 31). Sometimes people hurt us, and it is easy to harbour resentments which we can justify. However, resentments and grudges will only hurt us more. Let love, repentance, and forgiveness dominate and motivate our lives (Matt. 6:9–15; 1 Cor. 13). Once again, put the love of God at the top of your list of loves. But in the loving, do not forget to love yourself. The days of self-flagellating or self-denigrating Christians are long gone past, thank God.
- Just as tissues in the body communicate and give to one another, learn to be a giver. You will gain blessing from God as you do so (Acts 20:35; Luke 6:38). We live in a time when it seems important to seek pleasure and not miss out on the "fun things" of life. Television ads blast us with hedonism. You will not be happy unless you use a certain makeup, drive a certain car, drink a certain drink, and wear a certain type of clothing. We all know too well that these things do not make us happy. It is only God's peace which will make us happy and joyful

> as we live according to His plan (John 14:26–27; Matt. 5:3–12). We also need to give to ourselves. Golf is my recreation (it is a masochistic streak in me). The game helps recharge my batteries as well as keeping me reasonably fit. It is a great time to pray while you are in the bushes looking for your lost ball. Jesus also went into the wilderness to pray! My mother used to paint when her eyesight was good, and my ex-wife enjoyed folk art. It is all part of loving yourself.

My emphasis in this book has been on the nutritive and healing power of the Word of God as revealed to us by the Holy Ghost. God will, however, use other people in this healing process, just as He uses the medical profession to help heal our bodies.

I have used my experiences to illustrate how God moved in my life. As He healed my emotions, there was a lot of repentance followed by crying, which helped alleviate my emotional pain. God brought me into the path of Christian people who could help me at that time. As my innermost feelings were exposed to these Christian friends, they were able to help me just like various cells are involved in healing our damaged bodies. I am eternally grateful to God for their ministry to me in my hour of need.

God knows our needs better than we do. He will always make a way. He will shut the doors that need to be shut and open the right doors for us at the right time. It is important that we be healed and whole to help those around us. We must love and accept ourselves before we can love others. If we do not, then we need counselling. We need to pray that God will lead us to the right people who can help us. When you are healed, you will know. As Jesus said, "If you abide in My Word, you are my disciples indeed. And you shall know the truth, and the truth shall make you free" (John 8:31–32).

Finally, to be whole and healed in our Christian walk, we need to be truthful about our pain, in communication to God and to others, so that they may minister to us. The blessings and healing of God will be in our lives when we continually pray to and praise God, repent when needed, and have the Word of God in our hearts.

We must love God, our neighbour, and ourselves (Mark 12:30, 31). This three-part love and persistent study of the Word of God will give balance to our lives in both the physical and spiritual dimensions.

May God continue to bless and guide you in your walk with Him. In Jesus's name. Amen.

CHAPTER 7

MYTHS AND UNTRUTHS

In this chapter I have attempted to briefly answer, from a biblical and scientific perspective, various comments made to me over the years. Most of these topics have been touched on in the previous chapters of this book. I have called this chapter "Myths and Untruths" because that is what many of these comments are. They are perpetrated through the media and teaching institutions in our society, and need to be addressed.

Evolution explains everything, so one doesn't need creation by a God.

Evolution is the process describing how life forms progress from a microbe to a mouse to a monkey and finally to a man. A microbe has three million bases in its DNA, coding it functions and formation, whereas man has three billion, a thousandfold more. In biology, as in everything else, DNA breaks down or mutates in accord with the second law of thermodynamics. There is not one example in nature where a simple organism gains function by spontaneously adding a new gene. So to add a thousandfold increase in gene-mediated functions is absolutely impossible. In short, the process of evolution just cannot happen. Biological evolution is the biggest lie ever perpetrated. DNA degradation leads to death, not higher life forms.

> *The first life forms were born from chemicals in the environment interacting with one another.*

The DNA in a microbe has three million of bases that code for the functions and structures within the microbe. The four bases are designated by the letters A, C, G, and T, which can combine only in certain pairings. The bases have to be in right order for DNA to work, just as the words of this book must be in the right order and spelt correctly for you to understand what is written.

The probability of three million bases coming together in the right order in a microbe is $1/4^{3\ \text{million}}$, a very small number. Pragmatically, it is impossible. Bases are complex, cyclic, basic, aromatic structures and do not link together spontaneously. To link them, you need many complex proteins. To make those proteins, one needs not only DNA, but also hundreds of RNAs and proteins. So the probability of this happening gets smaller and smaller.

> *Rock strata indicate that the earth's geology formed over many millions of years.*

The rock strata indicate a massive worldwide flood, because the strata indicate they were laid down at about the same time. Otherwise there would be erosion as well as evidence of animal activity between the strata. Bends in the rock strata indicate they were laid down and bent while the rocks were wet and pliable.

The evidence from the eruption event at Mt St Helens indicates that a mini Grand Canyon, tens of metres high, can be formed in one day. There is additional evidence in our lifetimes that geological structures can be formed rapidly through catastrophic events (e.g., rapid island formation off the coasts of Hawaii and Iceland).

There are now two major schools of thought in geology. One is that everything formed gradually, which has been the prevalent view for about 150 years. This comes under the guise of historical science, because one would need to go back millions of years to confirm this process. The other view is that most geological formations can be formed catastrophically or in a short period of time. This belief is relatively new and can be confirmed scientifically. It has been borne out by the formation of new geological structure around the world, formed in less than a month.

The fossil record confirms evolution.

The fossil record is consistent with a worldwide flood. It also confirms that evolution is false, because there is no indication of intermediate life forms. Fossilisation only occurs when life forms are rapidly buried and slowly mineralised in soils, which would occur only in a flood situation.

Radioactive dating shows the world is billions of years old.

Unstable radioactive elements emit subatomic particles, which we can detect using measuring devices that count the particles emitted per unit of time. Radioactive disintegration for different elements is measured in a unit called a *half-life.* That is the amount of time radioactive element A takes to lose half of its radioactivity in its conversion to element B. The half-lives of some elements are millions or billions of years, whereas others are much shorter. Carbon-14 (C-14), the radioactive element used in carbon dating, has a half-life of 5,700 years and is undetectable after 100,000 years.

To age a rock or fossil, one must know the starting ratios of A and B. Many assumptions used in setting these ratios are ad hoc. Scientists assume, for example, that the starting amount of B is zero. Or they assume that the half-life is constant. There is evidence to show that the half-life can vary over time. Recent geologic events like the Mt St Helens eruption in May 1980 have resulted in the dating of rocks with ages well over a million years old, confirming that these ad hoc assumptions result in grossly inaccurate results.

Radioactive dating of rocks like diamonds and fossils using C-14 indicate ages of thousands, not millions, of years (C-14 has a relatively short half-life of 5,700 years and is undetectable after about 100,000 years).

Our universe is 14.6 billion years old, and our sun is 4.6 billion years old.

It is true that our universe is about fourteen billion light years in diameter. However, the Bible describes how God, in the beginning of time, stretched out the universe like a curtain, which means that in the beginning, all the galaxies were closer together. In fact, cosmologists have said our universe could fit in an area three million light years across, and there would still be a lot of space.

Our time/space dimension is sometimes described as a trampoline by those attempting to explain gravity. In the beginning, when galaxies were closer together, there would have been a huge mass and gravitational effect due to the relative proximities of these galaxies. Increased gravity slows time. In the beginning, clocks in the outer galaxies would have been trillions of time faster than earth time. This is one mechanism to explain how distant starlight could arrive at earth in the 6,500 years we know it to have actually existed.

Sure, Jesus Christ lived about two thousand years ago, but suggesting that he is God is a bit far-fetched.

Let us be honest about one thing. The New Testament makes it abundantly clear that Jesus is God and that He created this universe (Col. 1:15–17; John 1:1–4). His birth, death, and resurrection were prophesied hundreds of years before hHe came to earth. While on earth, over a three-year period, He performed miracles like raising the dead; healing blindness, leprosy, and deafness; changing water to wine; walking on water; and delivering people from demonic influences.

Scripture also prophesied that He would die for our sins, set us free from guilt by forgiving us our sinful state, and reconcile us to God the Father (Isa. 53:4–6). And Jesus made these claims while He walked among us (Luke 4:18, 19).

Perhaps the most convincing evidence that Jesus is God was when He rose bodily after His crucifixion (John 20:17). Jesus also sent His Holy Spirit to dwell with, comfort, and lead us, as He said He would (John 16:7, 8). Most Christians can testify to this. Those who know God can testify that the Bible is absolute truth—there is no lie in it. After all, it was inspired by God the Holy Spirit, and God cannot lie (2 Tim. 3:16, 17).

There are many religions that can lead us to God, not just Christianity.

Founders of other religions are all dead now, unlike Jesus Christ, who rose from the dead and is very much alive. A lot of gods other religions worship are mainly stone or clay idols. Jesus Christ is an actual, historical figure, and both secular and Christian scholars alike have documented this. Jesus Christ, who lived in Israel two thousand years ago, claimed exclusivity: He is the way, the truth, and the life, the only way to God the Father (John 14:6). In other words, there is no other way to God except through Jesus. Scripture and billions of current Christians testify that Jesus is alive. Christians in the past actually witnessed the risen Christ, with many paying with their lives for their belief. The Holy Spirit living within Christians makes us confident in this claim. Jesus alone has forgiven us our sins and reconciled us to our Holy God through His sacrificial death on Calvary two thousand years ago (Col. 1:20–22).

The process of evolution may have been how God created the world and would be consistent with the biblical claims.

God made it very clear in Genesis chapters 1 and 2 that He created the earth and all it contained within six twenty-four-hour days. God also emphasised that humans should work six days and rest on one day, just like He did when He created this earth (Exod. 20:11). Jesus also said that He made Adam and Eve from the beginning of time, not millions of years after creation of the earth (Mark 10:6). When God created this earth he said it was very good (Gen. 1:31). It could not be classified as very good if it consisted of animals tearing each other apart over millions of years of evolution.

Also, as previously stated, the process of biological evolution, from a scientific standpoint, just cannot occur. God would have to break His laws to permit it.

The Bible is very clear when it says that death entered the earth when humans first sinned (Rom 5:12–14). The genetics of mitochondrial DNA and the Y-chromosome indicate that we all came from one man and woman, and subsequently from the eight humans who remained after the worldwide flood in Noah's time.

If *Homo sapiens* had evolved between one million and 200,000 years ago, then we would have all died out long before now, given the mutation rate of our DNA and the number of mutations we hand on to the next generation.

Our lives do not count for much. We come here for around seventy-odd years, and then we die.

The Bible says that we are made in the image of God (Gen. 1:26). We have His creativity, logic, ability to love and care for others, and intelligence to achieve great things. We have His love of beauty and of the creation He designed. We also have the ability to worship and love our God. God has built this need for Him in us (eternity in our hearts) that He alone can fill (Ecclesiastes 3:11).

You may not be an Einstein or a Da Vinci, but you are unique in all of creation. There will never be anyone like you. God loves and values you to the extent that He gave his life for you at Calvary, so that you could be freed from your sins and spend an eternity of happiness with Him (John 3:16). The choice is yours, because in His love for us, He gave us free will. He did not make us robots.

> *Science has shown dinosaurs died out sixty-five million years ago when a huge meteor hit our planet.*

Recent research published in the journal *Science* showed the presence of intact biological soft tissue in dinosaur bones as well as the C-14 radioisotope. Soft tissue doesn't last sixty-five million years or even sixty-five hundred years. The presence of C-14 indicates dinosaurs probably became extinct a few hundred years ago. Sculptures of dinosaurs at Angkor Wat in Cambodia and at various sites around the world confirm that dinosaurs existed a few hundred years ago.

> *We can trust science because look what it has produced: drugs, immunisation, electronic gadgets, picture of our universe. So shouldn't we trust it when it shows that life has been here for a few hundred million years?*

There are two major forms of science, historical and experimental. The historical form of science has two worldviews, namely atheistic or Christian. When one sees a fossil in a rock, one uses a worldview to interpret its formation. An atheistic worldview would say that it formed a hundred million years ago. A Christian worldview would say it formed during the world flood in Noah's time about 4,500 years ago.

Historical science is storytelling, because we cannot rewind time. Christians, however, have the Bible to tell us what really happened, and the Bible doesn't lie.

Experimental science is different in that one does experiments, makes measurements, and obtains data. From this information, diseases are understood, better phones and computers are made, and so on. Many of the greatest experimental scientists were Christians.

So experimental and historical science are two very different sciences. Historical science usually relates to findings in geology and cosmology. One would have to time-travel back many thousands or millions of years to confirm the findings. But recent geological observations have confirmed that geological changes can occur catastrophically and not gradually over millions of years, as is currently taught.

The Bible is so complicated with rules and regulations.

In the Old Testament, there were many rules to do with sacrifices and foods, some allowable and others not. In addition, the Ten Commandments showed us how to live a moral and blessed life.

God selected a people, the Israelites, for Himself and His ultimate purpose of giving salvation—not only to them, but also to the rest of the world through them. The Ten Commandments and other rules were made for protection of Israelites and to set them apart from the rest of the world. These commandments highlighted humanity's sinful nature and our need of a saviour.

So the Ten Commandments were like a mirror to show us that we are sinful and basically could not meet the requirements of the law. Jesus told us that all we had to do was love God, our neighbour, and ourselves, and that all other commandments could be summed up simply by these three commands (Luke 10:27, 28). We are not to hold grudges against others but to have a loving attitude towards all. We are even to pray for our enemies.

Jesus knew our sinful nature and knew we could never be good enough to spend an eternity with an almighty and holy God. The Bible describes our righteousness as dirty rags (Isa. 64:6). For this reason, Jesus Christ took our sins to the cross of Calvary two thousand years ago to reconcile us to God. So we now have the righteousness of God through Christ's sacrifice and can be in the eternal presence of God.

To gain this right standing with God is very simple. First, admit to God that you are sinful by nature (i.e., a sinner) and repent of your sins. Second, thank Jesus for dying for your sins. Third, ask for and accept Jesus Christ into your life, to be your Lord and Saviour. You also need to repent of any satanic activities by rejecting Satan and his works. You can also ask Jesus to fill you with his Holy Spirit.

You are now a Christian. God will honour your prayer and begin working in your life to further sanctify you and make you more like Jesus. At this stage, the Bible will become more real to you because the Holy Spirit, now living within you, inspired the Bible (2 Tim. 3:16).

Finally, you need to ask God to direct you to a Christian church which stands on the Word of God. Such a church will help you understand God more fully and thereby help you grow in your spiritual walk with God.

Just realise that our salvation depends on whom we know, Jesus Christ, and not on what we know. One can have a PhD in theology and still not know Christ.

> *Christians are even confused because part of the Bible says we are saved by grace, whereas in another part works are emphasised.*

That is true to a certain extent. Most of the New Testament emphasises salvation through faith in the sacrifice of Jesus Christ, who took our sins to the cross. In other words, salvation is an unmerited gift from God, what we call *grace.* On the other hand, the epistle of James describes our works as being important (James 2:17).

The Bible is quite clear that our salvation is through faith in Jesus Christ. However, this faith requires us to do tasks that the Holy Spirit will motivate us to do. We Christians have a faith in Christ that works. So it is neither "faith and works" nor "faith or works," but "faith that works" (Eph. 2:8–10).

Jesus Christ and the Bible make many incredible claims about whom Jesus is. Can they be really true?

Jesus made many incredible claims about Himself. For example, He said:

- He and the God the Father are one (John 10:30, 38).
- He is the only way to salvation and eternal life (John 10:9, 3:16–18).
- He is the way, the truth, and the life (John 10:9).

In addition, many of His claims pointed to Him being God. For example, the Bible says that Jesus is God, who created the whole universe (Col. 1:15–17; John 1:1–4). What a claim!

So are all these claims about Jesus valid, or the claims of a lot of crazy people? The evidence would indicate that Jesus was truly all He claimed to be. For example, he performed incredible miracles, like curing all sorts of incurable diseases, raising the dead to life, calming the stormy seas, turning water to wine, feeding the five thousand on two loaves and five fishes, and so on. His most incredible miracle was that He rose bodily from the dead.

Also, scripture prophesied His virgin birth, place of birth, death, and resurrection hundred of years before the events. Many hundred of his followers were martyred because they believed in and saw His resurrected body after the crucifixion. If He was just a good man, I don't think people would be willing to die for Him.

In short, all the evidence points to Jesus Christ being God and to all the claims about Him in Holy Scripture being true.

If God is a God of love and compassion, how come there is so much heartache, suffering, and pain on earth?

It is true there is a lot of pain and suffering on our planet, and God, if He exists, doesn't seem to do anything about it. Atheists on this basis logically claim that there is no God.

To make sense of all this suffering, one needs to go to the early chapters of Genesis in the Bible.

In the initial creation, there was no pain or suffering. God said of His creation that it was very good (Gen. 1:31). However, Adam and Eve, because of their disobedience to God, introduced sin and death into this world, with all their associated pain and suffering. Humanity was subsequently cast out of the garden of Eden.

But God had a rescue package for us from the beginning, because of His love for us (Gen. 3:14, 15). He said that He was going to reconcile us to God and crush the originator of sin, namely Satan, the Devil.

To carry out His plan of rescue, God set aside a monotheistic people as His own. These were the Israelites, through whom our rescuer would come. That rescuer, called Jesus Christ, came as God promised, and was prophesied about hundreds of years before He came. Jesus reconciled us to God through His sacrificial death on the cross of Calvary, two thousand years ago (Col. 1:20–22; 2 Cor. 5:18, 19; Eph. 2:16).

As Christians, we all know that at death we will be in a place of peace with Almighty God forever (Rev. 21:1–4). We are also told in the Bible that there will be no more death, pain, suffering, or grief as we live with Jesus Christ (Rom. 8:18–21). As Christians, we also know that Jesus comforts and blesses us on earth as we daily walk with Him (2 Cor. 1:4–6; Matt. 5:4).

The Bible is about spiritual matters, and science is about the material world. So these disciplines should be kept entirely separate and not intrude on one another.

I used to believe this in the past. However, reading the Bible made me realise that this comment is completely untrue. The bible gives an historical account of life on our planet.

The Bible describes the order in which God created everything during creation week. It also describes the key early settlers and eras seen after creation. It makes one realise that the geological formations we see today were formed from a worldwide flood. It helps us understand, as confirmed by studies on mitochondrial and Y-chromosome genetics, that the human race is recent and less than six thousand years old. It explains how the civilisation spread and languages came about as a result of events after the tower of Babel. It explains how brother-sister marriages came about after creation, and how people in those days lived to almost one thousand years. It explains that the process of evolution is impossible.

In addition to all this scientific and anthropomorphically revealed evidence, the Bible also shows us how to grow spiritually and lead a life blessed by God. It shines light on the seriousness of sin and why Jesus had to die an horrific death to reconcile us to Almighty God. It shows us the depth of God's love for us.

Evolution occurs by natural selection allowing only those mutations it deems beneficial. Through this process, a simple life form (microbe) develops into more complex life forms.

Mutations over time lead to a degradation of the DNA code. Assuming there are so-called beneficial mutations, the question is how does natural selection select these?

First, natural selection can only detect gross changes called *phenotypes.* For example, natural selection says long-haired dogs survive longer in arctic conditions than hairless dogs. Wingless beetles do better on windy islands than beetles that depend on flight, because the latter group are blown out to sea. Natural selection cannot detect subtle DNA mutations and deem them beneficial or bad.

It is like you and your car. You cannot detect the rust occurring slowly under the paintwork until it spreads so much that it appears through the paint. You cannot detect the wear in the motor until you see blue-green smoke coming out of the exhaust. When you detect these gross changes, you as the selector can do something about your car—sell or repair it. The same is true with natural selection. Until the gross, external phenotype changes, there is no selection.

Printed in the United States
By Bookmasters